**WAR GAMES**

*ERRATUM*

The pictures on pages 116 and 164 have been transposed; the caption on page 116 refers to the picture on page 164 and vice versa.

# WAR
# GAMES

# WAR GAMES

## THE STORY OF SPORT IN WORLD WAR TWO

TONY McCARTHY

Macdonald
Queen Anne Press

A *Queen Anne Press* BOOK

© Tony Mc Carthy 1989

First published in Great Britain in 1989 by
Queen Anne Press, a division of
Macdonald & Co (Publishers) Ltd
66-73 Shoe Lane
London EC4P 4AB

A member of Maxwell Pergamon Publishing Corporation plc

Marbled cover pattern by Cockerell Marbled Papers of Cambridge.
Excerpts from *Mass Observation* copyright the Tom Harrisson Mass-
Observation Archive. Reproduced by permission of Curtis Brown Ltd.

**British Library Cataloguing in Publication Data**
Mc Carthy, Tony
    War Games : sport in the Second World War
    1. Great Britain. Sports, history
    1. Title
    796'.0941

    ISBN 0-356-17564-2

Typeset by MS Filmsetting Ltd, Frome

Printed and bound in Great Britain by Butler & Tanner Ltd, Frome

**Picture Credits**

Aldus Archive 57; Associated Press 22; Reg Auckland 155 (all); Mary Evans 13;
John Frost 46; Anthony Gross/Imperial War Museum 185; George Hahn 15 (top);
Hulton Deutsch cover, 18, 20 (both), 21 (both), 25, 26 (both), 27, 28, 30 (both),
37 (bottom), 44, 49, 50, 53, 55, 59, 65, 67, 68, 72, 75, 81 (top), 89, 91, 92, 95, 102,
105 (both), 106 (both), 109, 123 (right), 124, 125, 128 (bottom),132, 133, 134, 139,
154, 159, 161, 169, 170, 171, 178; Illustrated London News 64, 84, 88, 93, 144,
145 (top); Imperial War Museum 15 (bottom), 151; Lillywhites/Vintage Magazine
Company 79; Manchester Evening News 78; George Plumtre 176; Popper 35 (top),
41, 43, 45, 119, 130, 167, 172; *Punch* 58, 82, 103, 127, 131; Red Cross 86;
D C Thomson 16, 32, 35 (bottom); *The Times* 110; Topham 65, 100, 180;
Sport and General 115, 116, 164; *Sheffield Telegraph* 163; Major Slater 18;
*Yorkshire Post* 177.

# CONTENTS

# ACKNOWLEDGEMENTS

*Old men forget; yet all shall be forgot,*
*But he'll remember with advantages*
*What feats he did that day.*

William Shakespeare, *King Henry V*, Act IV, scene III.

Many of the letters received, in reply to requests for information in a wide range of papers and journals, simply stated that the writers had indeed forgotten, or become confused in their memories of, their participation in sport in wartime. Their wishes of good luck in the project were much appreciated. Others replied in considerable detail; it is noteworthy that although their experiences frequently overlapped in content — hockey in India, football leagues and athletics meetings in the Western Desert, Test matches in PoW camps — experiences rarely repeated each other, which is evidence of the wide spread and variety of events taking place. Perhaps there was a certain amount of 'shooting a line' in evidence in some of the stories, and elisions of time and place; why make do with a good tale if a better one can be constructed? However, documentary sources, God knows, can be as unreliable as verbal ones, even deliberately so.

My thanks, therefore, to all who contributed. For various reasons, I have not been able to contact all correspondents directly; I hope that those not specifically mentioned below will consider themselves included. I am grateful to all the editors who passed on my requests for assistance.

So, thanks to: Michael Alexander; Ian Askew; Joe Bacuzzi; Frank Renstead; H. Bell; Gwen Bickerton; Len Birkhead; Lt-Col. F.A. Bogie; E.F. Barbrooke; A.H. Brodhurst; John Bromhead; Gp-Capt. J.R.W. Blyth; Bobby Burnet; Douglas Burns; Bill Collyer; D.S. Colman; Neville Compton; Ron Craydon; S. Crighton; F.D. Crump; Stan Cullis; H.B.G. Dalgety; R.G. Davies; Dick Dawson; James Delot; Capt. R. de Norman; Ted Drake; G.K. Eames; E.T. Eley; Leslie Fairbairn; Harry Fenwick; David F. Forrester; D. Gibbs; James G. Gibson; R.M. Godden; Irene Gould; Jimmy Green; Gerald Gurney; Reg Gutteridge; F.W. Hales; Reg Hayter; Norman Hicks; David Higton; Dennis Hischier; Tony Hulley; Lilian Hunt; F.G. Jeavans; Thomas Jobling; Donald Jones; H.G. Jones; S.R. Kennerley; Air Vice-Marshal Larry Lamb; Dave Lanning; Johnny Leach;Mrs E.M. Lester; Jackie Loveday; Don McCorkingdale; Robbie McFarlane; Don MacIntosh; Mick McManus; Jean McPherson; Veronica Marchbanks; Sir Stanley Matthews; George Meadows; Chas Messenger; R.T. Milburn; Teresa Morris; Frank Mumford; G. Nelson; John Newcombe; J.M. Newby; Charles Nodes; G.A. Odell; Don Oliver; L. Palmer; Jim Parsons; Bill Peel; Norman Perren; D. Pike; Lord Porritt;

R.E. Porter; Les Preston; Netta Rheinberg; Ann Richmond; Lt-Col. T.M. Riddell; Rev. C.A. Roach; Jack Robertson; Cardew Robinson; T. Robinson; Mary Russell Vick; E. Schnabel; Harold Scott; Air Cdr. Peter Scott; Jack Seath; John Sheppard; Dorothy Sheridan; H. Simpson; Fred Skipper; Maj. L.E. Slater; Harry Slipper; R.P. Smith; F. Smithers; B. Stephenson; Alec Stock;·Dr. Richard Swann; Wing Cdr. Swallow; A.E. Taylor; Mrs M.G.S. Thresh; John Tyrrel; A.E. Waddoups; Johnny Walker; Harry Warren; Mel Watman; H. Watt; Barbara West; Bridget West; E. Westwood; E. Wilkinson; Jack Willett; the late Douglas Wilson; Fergus Wilson; Billy Wright; R. Wyatt; Maj-Gen. A. Yeoman; Fred Young.

In compiling the book, I could not have done without the help of Peter Delaunay and Bruce Reid (research); Paula Goodchild (secretary); Marion Milne and Malcolm Southan (LWT); Christine Davis and Elizabeth Loving (Queen Anne Press). I would also like to thank the International Red Cross and St John's Society for their help, and Collins publishers for permission to quote from Dan Maskell's *From Where I Sit*.

Every effort has been made to contact the owners of copyright material where known but without success in some cases, and copyright holders are invited to contact the publishers.

# INTRODUCTION

MY own affair with sport began after the war. I was – fractionally – a pre-war baby, and was evacuated to my grandparents' largish house in Stourbridge, Worcestershire soon after war broke out. Although there was a golf course next door, I have no memory of golf. In summer we used to wander round the golf course picking up strips of silver paper which had been dropped to confuse British radar, while in winter, for winters were real in those days, we would toboggan on tin trays down the fairways.

On summer evenings, my grandfather and his friends would send us to sleep with the clicking of bowls on the lawn. We found an old and cracked set in the summer-house, but since nobody explained bias, the results were not impressive. Our game consisted therefore of trying to knock the jack into the flower beds. As part of the war effort, the hard tennis court had been turned into a chicken run and the lawn court into a vegetable garden.

*War work. Behind the author and his mother, the tennis court became a chicken-run.*

Of organised sport there was only my grandfather's stories: how he had played rugby for Moseley and had toured Australia and New Zealand – there was the tail of a lyre bird on the wall to prove it, and a grass skirt removed from a Maori maiden. Uncle Denis, who had played cricket for Worcestershire (what was cricket?), was in North Africa and Italy (what were they?) and was the subject of many stories and, no doubt, silent worries. My father was also a rugby player and a good shot; it turned out later that he was a mean snooker-man too. However, we saw little of him as he stayed in the City of London police until, fed up with being bombed, he joined the RAF and was sent off to train in Canada.

Back in London after the war, we entered a new world of rapidly reorganised schools. And then came the Summer of '47, which introduced us to the Brave Old World of Compton and Edrich, Howarth of Worcestershire and Harold Butler, against whom Uncle Denis had batted.

The feeling of continuity returned. Perhaps, for sport's long-term good, it was too cosy. There had been major changes in the organisation of sport during the war, but the old order more or less re-emerged. The near-revolutionary mood of '45 was diverted by the summer of '47.

However, that's when the affair with sport started. It has mostly been a one-way process: I've been an inadequate hooker, a dubious left half, a hockey goalkeeper who let in 21 goals in two matches and an opening batsman who was originally put in there as a joke.

I've always had the gravest doubts about sport as an aid to moral quality, though many, especially those apparently in charge in 1939–45, probably disagree. But in terms of morale, sport played a role that was by no means less than the theatre, cinema, music and even the BBC. Jack, on the pitch, was as good as his master.

And that sort of spirit helped win the war.

# THE POLITICS OF SPORT

THE histories of sport and war have always been closely linked. The ancient Olympic Games, although originally a religious ceremony, soon incorporated an 'element' of athletics, starting with a simple stadium race to which other events were later added.

The Olympic festivities, celebrated every four years, were marked by a truce between the warring Greek states, called the *ekeheira*, which allowed participants to travel, train, compete and return home unhindered. The agreement for the cessation of hostilities was first organised by Iphitus of Elis in 884 BC and signed by the legislator of Sparta, Lycurgus, and the *archon* (chief magistrate) of Pisa, Cleosthcnes.

The notion of sport as a pacifying agent was thus born, although some of the later additions to the programme had military associations, notably javelin throwing and the *hoplite* race for heavily-armed soldiers. Huge crowds took advantage of the truce, coming from all over Greece and its colonies – Ionia, Italy, Sicily, Egypt, Libya and even the Dnieper – to watch the events.

The Olympic ideal was the attainment of beauty, to which every man of virtue should aspire. Beauty was seen as a mixture of strength, grace, courage, brilliance of mind and pure conscience. The Olympic champion was expected to embody all these qualities. This was not always the case, however. The philosopher and mathematician Pythagoras observed that three types of people mainly came to thc Games: athletes, stall-holders and the spectators. Of these he favoured the last – the athletes wanted glory, the stall-holders money, while the usually disparaged spectators at least came to enjoy the spectacle. Thc Olympic ideal was further diluted later, when the athletes became part of a touring professional circus. The Games were finally abolished in AD 393 by the Christian emperor Theodocius on the grounds of their paganism.

Throughout history, certain athletic events have been encouraged by military authorities. Fit, brave and skilled men were, of course, likely to make fine soldiers. Archery, swordsmanship and courtly jousting were favoured in mediaeval times, whereas the emerging rustic pastimes distinctly were not. Apart from generating public disorder (especially football), they hampered the various war efforts. In 1349 Edward III wrote to the Sheriffs of London complaining that 'the skill in shooting with arrows was almost totally laid aside for the purpose of useless and unlawful games'. Forty years later, Richard II forbade 'all playing at tennis, football, and other games called corts, dice, casting of the stone, kails and other such importunes games'. In 1423 James I of Scotland laid down that: 'It is statute, and the King

forbiddis that ne man play the futeball under the paine of fiftie schillings'. Such attempts to enforce the unenforceable naturally failed.

Even the modern Olympic Games owe their origin to a military consideration, despite the overt aim to bring the youth of the world together in peace and harmony. France had been overwhelmed by Germany in the Franco-Prussian war, and the freelance French patriot Baron de Coubertin came to Britain to see if he could trace what had made the Island Race so successful. He became convinced that 'since ancient Greece has passed away, the Anglo-Saxon race is the only one that fully appreciates the moral influence of physical culture and gives to this branch of educational science the attention it deserves'. He was deeply impressed by a Dr W. P. Brookes, who had organised for more than 40 years an annual 'Olympics' at Wenlock in Shropshire, with races for men and horses and some tennis and cricket

ABOVE *Greek* hoplite *soldiers. Races for the heavily-armed* hoplites *became a feature of the later Olympics, emphasising a connection between sport and war.*

RIGHT *An illustration from an Edwardian* Tom Brown's Schooldays *asserts the aggressive masculinity of the Public School sporting ethic.*

matches. He also admired the influence of sport and its ethics on English public schoolboys.

Despite the façade of peaceful internationalism, de Coubertin hoped that displays of excellence from the youth of other countries would eventually encourage the French to shake off their present torpor. One of his most persuasive arguments for reviving the Games was that encouraging the athletic spirit had a paramilitary value.

Religious appeal had its part to play as well: this was the great age of 'muscular christianity'. This movement derived largely from Dr Arnold's ap-

pointment in 1828 as the Head of Rugby School. Its effect was to turn public schools from the anarchy, disorder and brutality which had lately characterised them. The Rev. Mr Bowdler had called them 'the very seats and nurseries of vice'. If Waterloo had been won on the playing fields of Eton, it was not through any considerations of sportsmanship or fair play.

Arnold looked for '[first] religious and moral principle, second gentlemanly conduct, and third, intellectual ability'. Sport emerged as a bridge between these aims. Games were compulsory. The Royal Commission on Public Schools said that: 'the cricket and football fields are not merely places of exercise and amusement; they help to form some of the most valuable social qualities and manly virtues'.

As the century continued, the burgeoning (not to say bourgeois) new schools adopted the same principles. They also represented the world into which the recipients of these ideals were expected to go; to wars in the Empire against tribes who were basically disorganised, had little firepower and where skills of teamwork, dash and feats of daring and courage, implicit on the sportsfield, became essential. The Muscular Christians backed this with missionary work; the new Ideal Man was athletic, Spartan in his habits and totally patriotic. This was to mean that anything which smacked of effeminacy, intellectualism, or interest in anything foreign was not on course. Men like Charles Kingsley, Thomas Hughes (the author of the epitome of the Public School, *Tom Brown's Schooldays*) and the Rev. Leslie Steven (the Cambridge don and rowing coach) were prime propagandists for this new concept. Sport travelled the world with the bullet and the Bible.

The Olympic ideal of the 'whole man' had been divided. The aesthetes and the athletes – the 'arties' and the 'hearties' – had been set apart. The direct link between the playing field and the battlefield was clear, and the spirit of Sir Henry Newbolt's poem *Vitaï Lampada* (from the 'breath-less hush in the Close tonight' to the 'Red with the wreck of a square that broke') was not merely rhetoric, but a central part of motivation and belief.

The Forces, administrators and missionaries carried this British sporting ethic round the globe; sport helped bind the expatriates together, providing a common ground in strange places. It was also passed on to the native inhabitants as an alleged 'moral and civilising influence'. A third prong in this spread of British sport came from another area of British society – the working classes. Railway navvies and bridge builders, especially in South America and Eastern Europe, carried with them a game, Association Football. By the late nineteenth century, the game was fully developed: the Football Association rules had been established in 1864; professionalism (particularly in the Midlands and North, and at first involving Scottish 'professors' in the main) became accepted in the next couple of decades, and the Football League was established for the 1888–89 season. The rapid expansion of the railways in Britain meant not only that more distant fixtures could be fulfilled, but that crowds of supporters could be transported to them. To the surprise of the administrators, the working class did not spend their statutory Saturday half-day off fomenting radical political agitation, but playing and watching soccer. The authorities did not ignore the health and moral qualities of sport passed down to them from their colleges and schools; thousands of teams and clubs were set up around works and churches. One could well argue that sport was the opiate of the people.

When the First World War broke out, the 'muddied oafs' had a chance to put sporting ethics to the supreme test – on the muddier fields of battle. The England international, E. R. Mobbs, died leading a charge at the enemy lines, punting a rugger ball ahead of him, as if it were tacklers and not machine guns that faced him. The men followed. This was

ABOVE *Men from the East Surreys 'playing the game' and 'driving the trickling ball' at German WWI trenches.*

LEFT *Troops in Salonika playing soccer at Christmas in 1915; apart from relaxation, sport helped band together men from different backgrounds as a unit.*

by no means an unique case; soccer balls were used as well. Such heroics were well received at home, and a Mobbs memorial match is still staged today.

The rampant patriotic feeling back in England meant that organised sport at first had a rough ride. The County Cricket Championship spluttered on after the declaration of war on 4 August 1914. The title was awarded to Surrey, despite the fact that matches had been cancelled, and that they had to play Kent and Yorkshire at Lord's because the Army had taken over the Oval. The 1915 *Wisden* sighed that 'never before has the game been in such a plight', and Dr W. G. Grace commented in the *Sportsman* of 27 August 1914:

There are many cricketers who are already doing their duty but there are many more who do not seem to realise that in all probability they will have to serve either at home or abroad before the war is brought to a conclusion. The fighting on the Continent is very severe and is likely to be prolonged. I think the time has arrived when the county cricket season should be closed, for it is not fitting at a time like this that able-bodied men should be playing cricket by day, and pleasure seekers look on. There are so many who are young and able, and are still hanging back. I should like to see all first-class cricketers of suitable age set a good example, and come to the help of their country without delay in its hour of need.

There was no first-class cricket in 1915. Public feeling against it had been 'worked up to rather a high pitch', as Sydney Pardon, the editor of *Wisden*, observed. The football authorities decided to play on; Everton won the League in 1915 and Sheffield United the F.A. Cup.

The footballing authorities and players were subject to much criticism, not least from a Mr F. N. Charrington of the Mile End Mission, who called for a 'Footballers' Battalion'. The FA, who had their own dealings with the War Office, rejected these suggestions, and Mr Charrington started speaking out in condemnation of football. When he tried to do so in the interval of the Fulham v Clapton Orient match on 5 September 1914, he was ejected from the ground by Fulham's Chairman and Secretary. Charrington took them to court on a charge of assault, but lost; he was ordered to pay two guineas costs.

The Charrington view, however, *did* represent popular sentiment, against which the FA was

*In the First World War, footballers flocked to the Colours; this is a Bolton Wanderers contingent.*

powerless. A Footballers' Battalion was eventually formed as the result of a public meeting at Fulham Town Hall, and their first HQ was at the Richmond Athletic Ground. They became the 17th Service Battalion of the Middlesex Regiment. They first saw action in France in December 1915; Major Frank Buckley – later to become, with Wolverhampton Wanderers, one of the two most innovative club managers of the inter-war years – was wounded in shoulder and lung in 1916. He was for a long period their second-in-command. Another Footballers' Battalion was formed in 1915.

The feeling against sport was, in fact, grotesquely unfair. The sportsmen, as others, flocked to the colours. Before the end of the first month of the war, Croydon Common had twelve of their players in the Services; the club itself went into liquidation in 1917. And they paid, with others, the full price. One of the first professional footballers to be killed was John Wilson of the Vale of Leven and Dumbarton and the Black Watch in 1914. Second Lieutenant Donald Simpson Bell was posthumously awarded a VC for bravery in 1916 at the Somme. He had been a full back for Bradford. An early victim was one who had achieved a certain immortality, Lt A. E. J. Collins of the Royal Engineers, who gained a place in the record books aged 13 when he scored 628 out of 836 in a junior house match at Clifton College in 1899. Sixty pages of the slim 1917 *Wisden* were devoted to the obituaries of cricketers of greater or lesser fame, including half a dozen first-class players; many, no doubt, bought the attenuated Almanack in memory of a lost and loved one.

Sport readjusted; the traditional Football League was rearranged into Lancashire and Midland sections plus a 'London Combination' which was eventually to play a significant part in the organisation of soccer during the next war. There were various wranglings about payments and expenses for players and the division of gate-money. Police, after compulsory military service

was introduced in 1916, kept watch at football matches to spot malingerers.

Cricket strictly observed an MCC recommendation for counties not to play matches against each other, though the public schools – nurseries of future amateur talent – and the Marylebone Club organised 20 or 30 matches against them each summer. Also, the schools increasingly played matches against each other, rather than against clubs: Winchester, in 1915, met Harrow for the first time since 1854.

Anti-sport sentiment gradually subsided, at least partly from the realisation that sportsmen were not skrimshanking, and that sport had a part to play in raising money for war charities and to provide entertainment for war-weary and just-about-to-embark troops. Two matches at Lord's raised £1,300. One was between the English Army and the Australian Army (foreshadowing similar fixtures in World War II), which featured well-known players like Macartney and Kelleway for the Australians, with J. W. H. T. Douglas, Pelham Warner, Hendren, Tyldesley and Makepeace and Colin Blythe, the great left arm bowler, in his last appearance before he became another victim.

This retreat from jingoism and white-featherism is significant as regards attitudes to sport during the Second World War. So far as cricket went, the short gap between the wars meant that both administrators and senior players could present a justifiable case for its continuing, although in a modified form, from personal experience. Pelham Warner had captained charity teams in the first war and, acting as MCC secretary during most of the second, exemplified this continuity.

There was a sense of impotence amongst those at home during the First World War, which perhaps led to the animosity towards people actually enjoying themselves at such a time of struggle. In the Second World War, however, both civilians and services found themselves almost equally at risk. The need for rest and recreation applied to the whole country.

# THE LAST SUMMER

SPORT, until the first part of this century, had not been overtly regarded as a part of politics, as an arm of the State. It had been seen to have ethical, moral and social qualities which frequently coincided with the aims of Government, but was not generally regarded as part of a direct remit except insofar as it related to public health and order. Government, especially in Britain, was prepared to leave sport's organisation to voluntary and self-funding bodies. British success at sport derived from the kith and the kin; acceptance of sporting values followed from being British.

It was not until Nazi Germany that sport, health and fitness – in the Aryan mould – were brought together as part of a deliberate political programme. The German Weimar Republic had already spent sums of public money on sports equipment, arguing that sport could be a substitute for the military training that the Treaty of Versailles had put a tight rein upon. The coming to power of the Nazis did away with such subterfuges. In a deliberate reworking of the ancient Greek ideals, teamwork, comradeship and physi-

*Sport, representing the cults of physical perfection and success in the Aryan mould, was central to the training of the Hitler Youth.*

cal fitness were recharged with aggressive patriotism. Sports club members and work battalions alike were told that they were in effect already military men. Health and beauty were not just ideals; they were crucial elements of State policy.

In July 1935 a Dresden tennis team, the Blue-Whites, was banned from further progress in the National championships because a local Nazi offical thought that they had not sufficiently 'understood National Socialist ideology'. Jewish sportspeople were barred from all practice or competition – a move plainly against international Olympic tradition.

There were some slightly muffled protests: the president of the Maccabi World Union, an international organisation of Jewish sporting clubs, wrote an open letter to Count Henri Baillet-Latour, president of the International Olympic Committee (IOC), saying that, while he could not question the IOC's decision to keep the 1936 Games in Berlin, and sympathised with the idea of not mixing politics and sport, he

> in common with other Jews and many non-Jews, looked upon the state of affairs in Germany from the point of view of general humanity and social decency. We certainly do urge all Jewish sportsmen, for their own self respect, to refrain from competing in a country where they are discriminated against as a race and our Jewish brethren are treated with unexampled brutality.

However, only a handful of athletes from round the world did eventually boycott the Games. A plea for black American athletes to pull out went effectively unheeded, as did calls for a 'People's Olympics' or 'Workers Games' to be held in Barcelona. Avery Brundage, as president of the American Olympic Committee, thought that 'the active boycott by Jews and Communists' was even 'beneficial' since it had 'aroused the resentment of the athletic leaders, the sportsmen, and patriotic citizens of America and induced them to work harder, and to contribute more. It destroyed much

of the ignorance and apathy present in prior years'.

In Britain Harold Abrahams, the winner of the 100 metres sprint in the Paris Olympics in 1924, and a member of a distinguished Jewish family, vociferously headed off any call for a boycott. The General Council of the Trades Union Congress published a slim protest pamphlet calling for a campaign against the Nazification of German sport, called *Under the Heel of Hitler: The Dictatorship over Sport in Nazi Germany*, but it had small effect.

Sportspeople, especially in the West, have not generally been noted for their interest in political issues. (The Mexican 'black power' salutes in the Olympics of 1968 were highly untypical, deriving as they did from the athletes themselves rather than from outside organisation.) Most go along with the code of the day; they are fully occupied in exhausting routines of training, travelling and competition. The nearest they tend to come to political style activity is the occasional run-in with their sport's officials. This is not to say that they are stupid or immoral; they simply have a different set of priorities, and do not see why political considerations should interfere with what is either a profession or the means to achieving a lifetime's dream.

Much the same goes for the organisers of sports events, who have to plan future programmes, sit on international committees and actually run the activities. Those who encouraged participation in the 1936 Berlin Olympics, argued that sport *had* in fact contributed to a relaxation of international tension. After a confrontation with Hitler, who at first refused to alter 'a question of the highest importance within Germany ... for a small point of Olympic protocol', Baillet-Latour had forced him to take down anti-Semitic placards from the roadside on the way to Garmisch-Partenkirchen, where the Winter Games were held. Propaganda Minister Goebbels also toned down the overtly anti-Semitic campaigns. All this led to a naïve belief that anti-Semitism was simply part of the

ABOVE *The Berlin Olympics were a massive display, aimed at impressing the rest of the world; even anti-Semitism was reduced for the duration.*

LEFT *Despite his stylistic elegance, the German, Hans Sievert, did not win the Berlin decathlon. Americans took all three medals.*

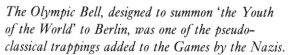
*The Olympic Bell, designed to summon 'the Youth of the World' to Berlin, was one of the pseudo-classical trappings added to the Games by the Nazis.*

*First and third placed, the Germans Schwarzmann and Frey celebrated their gymnastics victory with a Nazi salute. Switzerland's Mack did not.*

teething pains of the new and successful German state.

Hitler, in the euphoria of the Games, and German success, came to believe that athletes should be watched 'not as sportsmen, but rather as political troops who treat the sporting contests only as their particular branch of the great stuggle as a whole'. He also envisaged future Olympics taking place in a huge, 400,000-seat stadium. Albert Speer, his architect, pointed out that this would not be acceptable to the IOC, and would just be too big for conventional athletic events. The Führer brushed such considerations aside: 'In

1940, the Olympic Games will take place in Tokyo. But thereafter, they will take place in Germany for all time to come, in this stadium. And then we will determine the measurement of the athletic field.'

For the England football team, the existing Olympic stadium in Berlin was to present a moral problem. England were due to meet Germany on 14 May 1938, and, despite criticism, it was decided that the visiting team should, during the playing of *Deutschland Uber Alles* and the *Horst Wessel* song, give the Nazi salute. The Football Association judged that the raised arm was 'the national greeting of the country'. Sir Stanley Rous, then the Football Association Secretary, asked for advice from the British Ambassador, Sir Nevile Henderson on the matter. He replied: 'When I go in to see Herr Hitler, I give him the Nazi salute, because that is the normal courtesy expected. It carries no hint of approval of anything Hitler or his regime may do. And, if I do it, why should you or your team object?'

Several of the touring team were not at all happy with this attitude. One of the leading protestors, Stan Cullis, normally an automatic selection, found himself dropped for the German match and

*England's footballers giving the controversial Nazi salute before playing Germany in Berlin in 1938. It was excused as being 'a local custom'.*

the next against Switzerland, but was restored to favour for the following game against France. Stanley Rous was forced into the undignified position of begging 'I want you to do it for me'. Frank Broome, a forward on the trip, recalls the atmosphere: 'Jimmy Hagan, who had been coaching the Austrian team, translated the German papers, which were full of how the Germans were going to stuff it right up us. They were the master race. No one could beat the Reich.' Rous stressed tactfully that they must not lose for political reasons as well as sporting. England emerged 6–3 winners, much to the side's grim satisfaction.

Eddie Hapgood, the experienced Arsenal and England full back, later described his opponents on the day as a 'bunch of arrogant, sun-bronzed giants' just back from special training in the

Black Forest. Nevile Henderson had warned Rous about staging contests between German and British teams because the Nazis were looking for victories to boost the idea that the régime had produced a super race. The English victory clearly did not support that notion, and the next day a team from Aston Villa beat 'Greater Germany' (a German and ten Austrians) 3–2, introducing the Continent to the pleasures of the offside trap, which Villa's president later claimed was 'all a misunderstanding'.

Following an article surrounding the incident, the *Daily Telegraph* received two letters about hockey players' experiences in Nazi Germany. The first concerned Basil Brooke, whose father was at that time Treasurer to the Queen (now the Queen Mother). Following his selection for the team at the German university he was attending, he was advised by the Palace that on no account should he give the Nazi salute when lining up for anthems – or indeed any other occasion. He was told that, as a former member of the Winchester College OTC, he should use the British Army salute. The other letter was from Mr R. A. Child, who recalled:

> When I toured south Germany in April 1937 in a public school hockey team ... we did not warrant bands and anthems but simply lined up midfield and after the *Seig Heils* and salutes, we countered by brandishing our sticks in the air and yelling 'Whipsnade, Whipsnade, Zoo, Zoo, Zoo'. This never failed to raise a tremendous roar of approval from the not inconsiderable crowds which followed our progress wherever we went.

There was, then, little overt anti-British feeling in the German sports world as late as 1938. In fact many Germans felt they still had a great deal to learn. In August the Somerset Wanderers cricket team played against a Combined Berlin XI, and were held to a draw. The result might have been affected by the previous night's hospitality provided by Herr Henner Walter and Herr Boos. The tour organiser, Felix Menzel, a leading figure in German cricket, urged the British to encourage the game on the Continent, advocating an international cup competition involving an MCC team and sides from Germany, Belgium, Holland and Denmark. It would give, he said, a wonderful impetus to cricket on the Continent, and would provide an opportunity for British and Continental players to get to know each other.

Menzel's was a remarkable speech, involving the continuing notion of sport as an international emollient and the revolutionary concept of an international cup. Had it not been for the War, there is every chance that (MCC allowing) such an event could have taken place. As it turned out, cricket in Holland and Denmark became a symbol of resistance to German occupation.

Sport thus went on in its accustomed way, by and large. Plans continued for the next Olympic Games, due for Tokyo in 1940. Japan was already engaged in military campagins in Asia, and petitions were being started to change the venue. Avery Brundage, still President of the American Olympic Committee, continued to assert that 'sport transcends all political and racial situations' and that 'whether our Committee or athletes like or dislike Japan's military policy is beside the point'. The emerging Japanese ruling elite itself, however, scorned the apparently peaceful Olympic ideal as being contrary to the spirit of the 'Bushido' code of the traditional Japanese fighting aristocracy. On 12 July 1938 Japan withdrew the Olympic invitations. Amid some confusion, Finland was picked as the second home of the XII Olympiad.

Britain did not remain totally unmoved by Continental developments; the response was a typical combination of voluntarism and government-inspired 'action' that smacked of bureaucracy. The National Playing Fields Association had been set up in 1925, with the Duke of York (later King George VI) addressing the inaugural meeting. Women's keep-fit organis-ations sprang up, the chief body being Mrs Bagot Stack's Women's League for Health and Beauty, founded in 1929. The Youth Hostel movement, in clear imitation of the German model, started in 1930, and there were organisations, often with left-wing and radical connections, for camping, canoeing, cycling and rambling. Yet there was a worry in general about post-school-age provision and leadership. Most of the governing bodies were adult- and competition-orientated. The King George Jubilee Trust was set up in March 1935, and Lord Portal, its vice-chairman, was shortly to write of 'large numbers of boys and girls who are approaching the age of full citizenship ill-equipped for the responsibilities which face them – and this at a time when it is clear that the manhood and womanhood of this nation may yet be tested as never before'. Kurt Hahn – founder of Gordonstoun School – spoke of 'the contentedly unfit youth of today' and 'the sloth of modern adolescence'.

Meanwhile, the Central Council of Recreative Physical Training (CCRPT), the brainchild of Phyllis Colson, a physical education teacher and inspirational organiser, was set up on 4 July 1935. It was a mixture of governing bodies' representa-tives and other interested parties, including, apart from sport, dancing and keep-fit. Such was the concern about the fitness of the nation that 14 of the original 34 members of the Council were from the medical profession.

The British Medical Association's Physical Education Committee produced in April 1936 an important report endorsing the activities of the CCRPT in a wide-ranging and still often valid look at the social advantages of PT. The Govern-ment were anxious not to appear to be echoing totalitarian ideals, but felt they ought to be seen to be concerned with an issue that had struck public awareness – and it naturally produced a White Paper, in January 1937, *Physical Training and Recreation*. It set up a Fitness Council to run a National Fitness Campaign; the Secretary was Captain Lionel Ellis, and Chairman, Lord Aber-dare, formerly C. N. Bruce, a distinguished cricketer and tennis player. The membership of the Council was star-studded and included Philip Noel-Baker, M. P., Lord Burghley, A. E. Fern from swimming, Stanley Rous and W. W. Wake-field, but only two professional physical educa-tionalists, A. H. Gem from the LCC and Phyllis Spafford from the Ling Gymnastic Association. A Physical Training and Recreation Act, establish-ing the Council, became law in July 1937.

The King had become patron of the CCRPT, and attended with the Queen and his two young daughters a Festival of Youth at Wembley in that month. The CCRPT report emphasised that its success showed that 'the co-ordination of many organisations results in a pleasing emphasis of their individuality, rather than that subordination to uniformity which is sometimes so acutely feared'.

The NFC had some limited successes, includ-ing 'Fitness wins', 'Get fit – keep fit' and 'Daily Dozen' poster, leaflet and film campaigns. Some facilities in different localities were funded, but it never managed to establish its proposed National College of Physical Training in Merstham, Sur-rey. Its bright young officers upset existing local authorities, and seemed at arm's length sometimes from the CCRPT. The NFC was one of the war's first casualties; it went out of business unhonoured and unsung, with scarcely an obituary notice.

The sports world thus drifted into 1939; there were no special plans made, no alternative fixtures organised. In that this reflected the apparent national position in general, no blame can be cast. Although air raid precautions had been stepped up and there were complaints against the slowness of British rearmament, there remained a belief that 'the storm of war, if it came, would blow east-wards, against Soviet Russia'. That sports organis-

*The West Indians were the last pre-war cricket tourists to England. Clarke, Martindale and Constantine were to return for wartime games.*

ations made little preparation for their future might, with hindsight, appear surprising; however, the government itself was still toying with the idea of a conference, instigated by Mussolini, as late as 2 September 1939, the day before the declaration of war on Germany.

Sport therefore continued more or less as normal during the summer of '39. The English cricketers had returned from a winter tour of South Africa which remained tantalisingly undecided. Walter Hammond's team were 1–0 up in the series when the sides met for the final Test at Durban which, it had been decided, was to be played to a finish no matter how long it took. Ten days later the now legendary 'Timeless Test' was still incomplete and the game had to be abandoned

as a draw to enable the England team to catch their boat home. Bill Edrich, with 219 in that Durban match, established himself at international level. England were in the process of building one of their potentially strongest-ever teams. Despite his South African success, Bill Edrich could not command a Test place. The summer tourists were the West Indies, captained by Cambridge Blue R. S. Grant.

Four years earlier, the West Indies had won their first series, at home, by 2–1, with a crushing victory by an innings and 171 runs in the last Test.

*Learie (later Lord) Constantine, backed by K. H. Weekes, is in formal mode during the 1939 tour.*

BELOW *Two of the great West Indian players of 1939, E. A. 'Manny' Martindale (left) and George 'Atlas' Headley.*

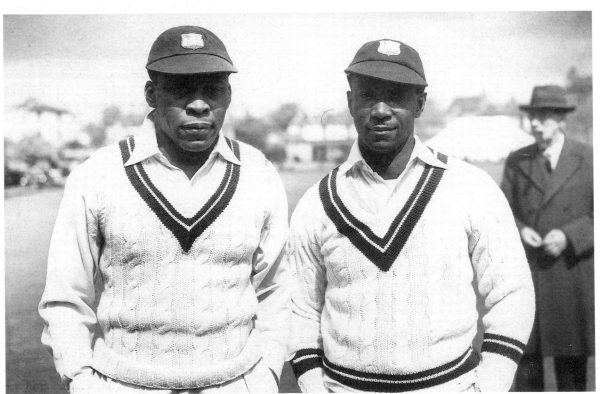

George Headley scored 270 in this rout at Kingston, Jamaica. Nicknamed 'Atlas', he certainly carried the West Indies main batting hopes in the Thirties, helping them to their first ever Test victory in 1930. Nor was the bowling to be sniffed at; had he been able to play more Test cricket E. A. 'Manny' Martindale would have had a high place in the Caribbean fast-bowling roll of honour. As a professional, he played much northern league cricket as did Learie Constantine, the team's leading all-rounder, who became a much-travelled

*England's regular goalkeeper before the war, Vic Woodley (Chelsea) greets Sam Bartram (Charlton), a wartime favourite.*

favourite during the war. Leg-spinner C. B. Clarke was also to become a leading figure in wartime cricket. But the 1939 summer saw a series victory for England, based on a win at Lord's in the First Test, with centuries from Len Hutton and Denis Compton, two young men who where on the way to making themselves national heroes. The medium-paced bowler, Bill Copson, from Derbyshire, with nine wickets in the match, had no glamorous aspirations, but contributed as much. The two other Tests were drawn, a low-scoring one at Manchester and a high-scoring one at the Oval, where Constantine thrashed England for 70 out of 103 added in only an hour. These West Indies were no mean team, but they had to

wait until 1950 for the first touring Test series in England to be won. Curiously, it was not their then pacemen who did the damage, but the spinners, 'those little pals of mine – Ramadhin and Valentine'. But for the war, a similar result might have happened even earlier; certainly an understrength England team was hammered in the Islands in 1948. Even bringing over Hutton as a reinforcement did not ensure victory.

Meanwhile, England's soccer players embarked on a spring tour in areas which must have been considered sensitive, to say the least. A team containing Woodley in goal, Hapgood, Cullis, Mercer, Matthews, Goulden and Broome, toured Italy, Yugoslavia and Rumania (the last full international till they played Northern Ireland in 1946). In Milan, they drew 2–2; in Belgrade, they lost 1–2, and they picked up a 2–0 win in Bucharest. It seems that the Foreign Office had some worries about the tour, but the players themselves, isolated from much public contact, appear to have been more amused than alarmed by security fencing.

At Wembley, Portsmouth scored an unexpected and thumping 4–1 victory over Wolverhampton Wanderers, with goals from Parker (2), Barlow and Anderson. As the 'Pompey Chimes' rang out, the club probably could not have guessed that, by default, they were to hold the FA Cup for longer than anyone else. In the League, Everton took the title with 59 points, fairly comfortably ahead of Wolves (55 – and in runner-up position for the second consecutive season) and Charlton Athletic (50 points).

The customary events of the summer unrolled more or less normally. 16,000 paying customers watched Oxford play Cambridge at Lord's, though Headquarters was the scene of a distinct

*LEFT Portsmouth supporters, Up For The Cup, arriving at Waterloo for the Final against Wolverhampton Wanderers. Their team's win surprised almost all.*

'unpleasantness' after the Eton v. Harrow match. Harrow won for the first time since 1908 and there was 'delirious excitement'. Some 8,000 people cheered and fought in front of the pavilion, and there were rumours that the fixture would be discontinued.

It was the Henley Royal Regatta's centenary year, and the Stewards managed to persuade a strong Harvard squad to come over. They took their training very seriously, eschewing the nightlife on their liner, the *Normandie*, and obeying the instructions of their coach, the professional Tom Bolles, who had to learn in a short while the skills of operating from a bicycle and through a megaphone on the towpath.

This was the England of a dream; an England for which many thousands of countrymen were to fight and die. The American visitors, who included Thames Cup winners Tabor Academy (beating Kent School), were delighted by the colourful oars, the tents, the hospitality, and the rowers from present and long-past. The president of the Union Boat Club in Boston wrote feelingly, on his return, in the official rowing guide: 'Just when we may see it all again no one knows. Our wish and our hope is that it may be soon'.

Sport's organisers showed a clear intention to continue as normal during the summer of 1939, with a grim determination that from our angle looks almost perverse. The IRA was perceived as the chief threat, since that was immediate and local. The boat tents at Henley had a sprinkler system and were 'under guard'. At Epsom in Derby week, 'special secret precautions' were taken, as the official communique had it, to 'prevent the success of any attempt by Irish political extremists to interfere with racing'. The press still concerned themselves with what now seem trivial issues – the state of the going at Goodwood (which survived a drenching on the Monday, but recovered magnificently on the next day); the resourcefulness of the police in handling the traffic; and the fashions at the meeting

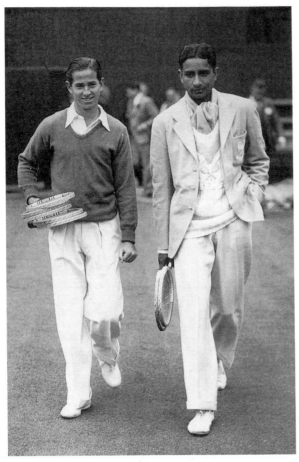

LEFT *Americans were involved in all the victories in the last pre-war Wimbledon: coming onto court are the Indian J. Dhamija and Bobby Riggs.*

BELOW *Kay Stammers was beaten by Alice Marble in the women's singles final.*

('Well up to Ascot standard,' opined *The Times* correspondent. 'The Honourable Mrs Micklethwaite's stone-coloured dress was matched by her fox cape, and her close-fitting cap of brown straw was edged with gold *galon*'.) Clothes rationing and newsprint shortages were soon to put an end to that sort of dressing – and writing.

Wimbledon was dominated by Americans, despite Donald Budge moving to the professional ranks. Bobby Riggs – now probably better known for his preposterous challenge, in his old age, to Billie Jean King – and Alice Marble each achieved a hat-trick. They won together in the mixed doubles; in the men's doubles he played with Ellwood Cook, whom he beat in the men's final, and Marble joined with Sarah Palfrey Fabian to win the ladies' doubles. Britain had, once again, flattered to deceive. Hare and Wilde reached the men's doubles final; Nina Brown joined Wilde as losing mixed finalists, as was Kay Stammers in the ladies. In the light of what was to follow, was the absence of Gottfried von Cramm a sinister portent?

Dan Maskell, now the doyen of BBC commentators, recaptured his British professional singles and doubles titles. In his memoirs, he recalls what must have been the experience of many full-time sportspeople:

As the summer faded there was more and more talk in the papers about the possibility of war. Since I had been kept pretty busy all the year I had not really given the matter much thought. But as the speculation intensified my mind went back to an incident at Wimbledon. A few days after the end of the Championships Jean Borotra (the Frenchman) had come down to the club for a game with me. As he was putting his belongings together prior to his departure he had seemed unusually serious, sad almost.

Turning to me with that earnest look he always has when he is feeling emotional, he said, 'Dan, I want to send you something with all my thanks for the many years you have been helping me here. You know it may be a very long time before we see each other again.' Some weeks later a silver cigarette case, suitably inscribed, was delivered to my home. By then, it was already clear that Jean had been right.

Cricketers had been coming to a similar conclusion. It had been an interesting summer, and the writer R. C. Robertson-Glasgow, looking back on it, reflected that 'as is customary when great issues hang in the balance, men set themselves to quiet but determined enjoyment'.

On 24 August the Kent secretary, G. de L. Hough, suggested to the West Indians that their match projected for the 30th might have to be cancelled because of the deepening crisis. The tourists hastily packed their bags and sailed from Glasgow two days later, leaving officials at Sussex, where the tourists were due to play, huffing and puffing. Sir Home Gordon said that 'indignation was profoundly excited' and A. J. Holmes wired them on the 25th: 'Essential to keep the flag flying'. Most people sympathised with their desire to get home to their families, and the journey itself proved perilous enough.

The first class cricket played on Wednesday, 30 August to Friday, 1 September was the last until after the war. Lancashire played Surrey at home because the Oval had already been designated as a potential prisoner of war camp (for expected German parachutists). The two teams agreed to call the match off as a draw in Surrey's favour after two days, so that the players could get back to their homes. Middlesex beat Warwickshire at Lord's. This match was the subject of one of Neville Cardus' wilder flights of fancy. Watching some desultory cricket on the Friday, with a long barrage balloon hanging overhead, he saw workmen removing the bust of W. G. Grace, to put in a place of greater safety. 'The noble Lord at my side,' wrote Cardus, 'watched their every movement; then he turned to me. "Did you see that, sir?" he asked. I told him I had seen. "That means war," he said.'

Since the match had ended the previous day, and Cardus was in Australia at the time, the story has a ring of poetic licence. However, the treasures of Lord's were soon to be taken away and stored. With the cancellation of the Festival matches and the planned Indian tour, the war had indeed started to make its mark on cricketers. Ironically, the popular Worcestershire amateur all-rounder, R. H. C. Human, had been picked for that tour and was to become that county's only war casualty. England's women cricketers, despite having saved up for months to make the trip, and to buy smart new team clothing, also had to call off their planned tour to Australia.

Yorkshire travelled to Hove from Bournemouth

*Bolton Wanderers in uniform, 1939. From left to right: Jack Ithell, Danny Winter, Jack Roberts, George Catterall, Don Howe and Harry Goslin. The team enlisted virtually as a unit.*

for their final fixture. A chief factor in the decision to complete the programme was that this was Jim Parks' benefit match. Despite damp weather, the visit of Yorkshire was expected to raise a good crowd, for there were still plenty of holiday-makers in Brighton. The first two days were high-scoring. George Cox made 198 out of Sussex's 387. Centuries from Len Hutton (103) and Norman Yardley (107), the future England skipper, gave Yorkshire a five-run lead. But then came the rain, turning an amiable pitch into a nightmare track. The great Hedley Verity, slow left-arm, was able to exploit it to the utmost. Renowed for his skill and resources on the best batting wickets against the world's finest players, Verity, given this sort of chance, was unplayable. He took seven wickets for nine runs in six overs, keeping himself,

with 191 wickets at 13.13, clearly at the top of the national averages. Yorkshire needed 29 to win, and though Hutton went for one, Yorkshire won comfortably by nine wickets.

Play finished at 2.30 on Friday, 1 September 1939, and the Yorkshire cricketers made their way sombrely home by charabanc, because they were not allowed to use cars south of Birmingham and the trains were crowded with evacuees. Many wondered if they would ever play again. Len Hutton was reported as looking 'serious' and 'very pale'. They spent a short night in Leicester, not even bothering to unpack their overnight gear, and were home by mid-day on the Saturday. Len Hutton hurriedly brought forward his wedding to Dorothy Mary Dennis, due to take place in October, to 16 September. Movietone and Pathe News were in attendance.

Cricket had not specifically ignored the portents of war, nor had it made plans for its future. During the Lord's Test, Walter Hammond had appealed over the loudspeakers for men to volunteer for national service, and the stands carried hoardings asking 'National Service – Are You Playing?' The question of what specific function sport itself was going to play, seems to have been entirely overlooked.

Much the same applied to soccer – footballers returned to train for a new season in an entirely unreal atmosphere. Many had already joined the Territorials and other services to 'do their bit'. A Football Association circular of April 1939 hoped that the game would provide a patriotic example to the youth of the country. And so it did. Some clubs volunteered virtually *en masse*. Brentford joined the War Reserve Police and learned the basics at their home ground, Griffin Park. Liverpool, including manager George Kay and assistant secretary Jack Rouse, chose the Territorials; Bolton Wanderers and West Ham enlisted virtually as a unit.

With the call-up increasingly demanding the services of reservists, clubs worried about having to pay players who were not actually performing. In July, the League Management Committee's minutes noted that 'there is no onus on clubs to pay players called up for military service during their period of military training. If, however, arrangements can be made with the military authorities for the players' services on match days, then liability would arise during such week or weeks as the players are available for the club'. Understandably, since the conscription was for six months, they hoped that footballers' liability would be reduced to four months, preferably

during the summer.

Nonetheless, the League programme did restart as scheduled on 26 August, attracting 600,000 spectators, down on average figures for the opening day. Midweek matches followed and, despite the evacuation of children from 1 September, and Friday's invasion of Poland, the Home Office issued a bulletin saying that the situation did not demand the cancellation of matches. Only 380,000 spectators attended. Arsenal kicked off against Sunderland at 5 pm, and Fulham an hour later because of likely crowd and traffic problems. Liverpool only got a team together because some of their Territorial mates offered to take over sentry duty for seven of the players. The highest scorers were Bournemouth, who beat North-ampton 10–0, but only after the Chairman's son had been recruited to run the line when the appointed official did not turn up. Blackpool, with three wins, headed the League.

But these efforts to create an air of normality foundered when war was declared on 3 September. An automatic ban on the assembly of crowds came into effect; and sport came to a halt.

*Sport stopped indefinitely on the declaration of war. Headline from the* Daily Mail, *4 September 1939.*

# ALL SPORT BROUGHT TO A HALT
## Restart When Safe for Crowds

# EARLY WAR

THE French followed suit at 5 pm, without any special enthusiasm – the declaration of war had been primarily a decision of the British parliament. Other states fell variously into line.

Britain's declaration had automatically involved India and the colonies; the Dominions – now free to choose for themselves – differed in their responses. Australia and New Zealand took Britain's lead without reference to their parliaments; Canada did consult, and declared war on 10 September. Herzog, South Africa's prime minister, wanted to remain neutral, but parliament resolved on war by 80 votes to 67; the governor general refused a dissolution, and Smuts became prime minister. De Valera's Irish Republic stayed resolutely – if contentiously – neutral. There was no evidence of the fanciful 'world crusade for freedom and against fascism' which became later a popular notion in some circles; after all, two great powers, the Soviet Union and the United States, only took up the cudgels after they themselves were attacked. The British people, if anything, were probably surprised at the noble part which events had thrust on them, as the historian A. J. P. Taylor has pointed out. There was none of the war fervour which had gripped Britain in 1914. The mood was grim, determined if need be, cheerful where possible, and taken with a deepening per-plexity when the war turned out to be, at first, very unlike what had been anticipated.

As regards sport, the immediate effect was 'a knock-out blow, a complete scattering of the sport world to a standstill', according to H. J. Novy, a young reporter on the team of Tom Harrisson's pioneering social survey, *Mass Observation*. Novy summed up the situation:

> The war broke the spell of sport, swept away steeple-chases, greyhounds and all-in, bowls and archery, fencing and tennis. The magic habit of recurring matches and pools and all that the other elaborate weekly cycles brought out in the press, was broken. As anthropologists know, the breaking of an established habit which recurs at regular intervals, can have deep repercussions. People become 'conscious' of what they are doing instead of taking it for granted each week as an essential part of the routine of living.

*Images of early war.* ABOVE RIGHT *evacuees from West Ham wait to be allotted to their new homes at Truro, June 1940; whilst* RIGHT *Brentford FC players take an early instruction in gas masks. Brentford joined the police* en bloc *at the outbreak of war.*

Novy, writing from October 1939 to January 1940, appreciated that sport was more than an entertainment, to be sacrificed in an emergency; it was a central part of everyday existence. Virtually nobody had realised that it was something to be preserved, even nurtured, and the vast majority of people took its disappearance with the bewildered calm of a people whose world had just been turned upside-down.

Within weeks of the blanket ban on sport, however, ad hoc and later more organised events were being staged. War had not turned out to be, at first, anything like what was generally expected – no gas, no trenches, no blitzkreig – and sport came out of its shell. New war-time competitions and friendly matches were born. Many admittedly were of a makeshift character – it was not a time for long-term plans, but 'make-do', in sport as elsewhere.

The immediate reaction of the football authorities was a mixture of the confused and draconian, but with an eye to commercial considerations. On 5 September, the Football League president, W. C. Cuff, announced that clubs should retain their players on contract to stand by, but an emergency meeting of the Management Committee at Crewe the next day reversed that decision. It was also decided that season ticket refunds could not yet be given, and the Committee deferred alternative schemes for competition when soccer resumed. The Scottish FA, in Glasgow, suspended all contracts between players and clubs; two days later 15 representatives of the League and FA met at Lancaster Gate as the War Emergency Committee.

The Committee decided that all football except for the Forces, under the jurisdiction of the Association, would be suspended until official notice to the contrary was given. Furthermore, all players' contracts were suspended – putting them out of a job, though the clubs hung onto the players' registrations. The FA quickly offered the services of coaches, trainers and masseurs to the Forces, while clubs offered their grounds and amenities for recreational purposes. The FA made its first donation, of £1,000, to be spent on footballs and other equipment for the Army. The following afternoon QPR played the Army behind closed doors and a scratch QPR team (comprising those who were not on Metropolitan Police duty since the team had enlisted *en masse*) beat their opponents 10–2.

Regional competitions were being considered, and the Players' Union offered to allow its members to play for nothing, if the money was given to charity. The League Management Committee said that no payments to players could in any case be made, but that they would be insured under the Work Compensation Act. Shortly afterwards, it was announced that friendly matches could be played even in those areas where football was banned by the Home Office, should the local police approve. On 21 September, after consulting the Home Office, the FA announced that it would lend its full support to friendly and competitive matches on Saturdays and public holidays, so long as there was no interference with the National Service or the war effort.

Crowds were generally limited to 8,000, or 15,000 for grounds with a capacity for 60,000, and these were to be all-ticket matches, sold in advance. On 16 September, some 31 first-class friendlies were held, on an amateur basis, in front of 120,000 spectators. There were some high scores and some upsets, with Midland League Peterborough doing a preliminary spot of giant-killing, beating Nottingham Forest 4–3. The *Yorkshire Post* admitted that while wartime soccer 'would lack the keenness and excitement of League competition, there was the opportunity for spectacular exhibitions, with skilful manoeuvres and finesse to be exploited, enabling players to display whatever ball craft they possessed'. Unfortunately, Halifax v Leeds was at a level 'usually associated with the village green'.

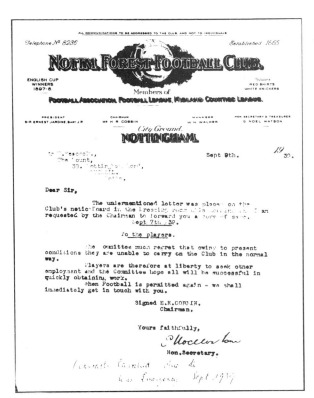

NOTT'M FOREST FOOTBALL CLUB.

Telephone Nº 8236                                    Established 1865

ENGLISH CUP
WINNERS
1897-8
                    Members of
FOOTBALL ASSOCIATION, FOOTBALL LEAGUE, MIDLAND COUNTIES LEAGUE.

Colours
RED SHIRTS
WHITE KNICKERS

PRESIDENT          CHAIRMAN          MANAGER          HON. SECRETARY & TREASURER
SIR ERNEST JARDINE, BART.J.P.   MR H R COBBIN     W H WALKER           G NOEL WATSON

City Ground,
NOTTINGHAM.

                                Sept 9th.        19 39.

Dear Sir,

        The undermentioned letter was placed on the
Club's notice board in the dressing room of the first team and I am
requested by the Chairman to forward you a copy of same.
                Sept 7th. 39.

        To the players.

        The Committee much regret that owing to present
conditions they are unable to carry on the Club in the normal
way.

        Players are therefore at liberty to seek other
employment and the Committee hope all will be successful in
quickly obtaining work.

        When Football is permitted again - we shall
immediately get in touch with you.

                Signed H.R.COBBIN.
                        Chairman.

        Yours faithfully,

                Hon. Secretary.

LEFT *The first reaction to war was to cancel footballers' contracts (though registrations were retained). A fairer compromise was soon reached.*

BELOW *Servicemen, often removed from their regular haunts, were eager to watch sport wherever they could find it.*

The Topical Times *looks light-heartedly at some footballers' wartime occupations. It was important for morale that sportsmen should be seen to be taking part.*

Spectator reaction was variable. A 48-year-old London park-keeper noted, for *Mass Observation*, in his diary (30.9.39):

Fulham have a wartime friendly match; I decide to go. There is as yet no decision on resuming ordinary League football. The Government or police have limited the crowd to 8,000, so tickets are issued at the turnstiles as you pass in. When these tickets are exhausted, the gates are closed. The number however was, guessing, well below 8,000. I should say 5–6,000. Rather a poor game which evoked sarcastic but topical remarks from the noisy element of the crowd. To a forward who misses an open goal 'Take your gas mask off', 'Ref, blow the siren and let us take cover' and other caustic comments. For me, however, although not a brilliant game, I found enough good play to satisfy me; an afternoon's diversion.

A Blackburn fan was not so impressed; though he was prepared to travel as a neutral:

Sat. Oct. 7. Preston v Bolton. Very disappointed at the football match. Walked round the ground before the kick off, but did not hear one single comment on the war, was surprised to note that there was practically no conversation at all; general impression of listlessness, very unlike the usual football crowd.

Sat. Oct. 14. Blackburn v Bury. Noticed very few soldiers at the football match, in fact only about 1,000 were there in all, counted only six civilians carrying gas masks.

(This correspondent was obviously a responsible citizen, for he complains later about 'very few gas masks at the match' – carrying them to such events was in theory mandatory – and again the failure of the fans to talk about the war: 'no comments at the football match except about football'.)

On 22 September, it was agreed that professionals in England would receive no more than thirty shillings for each match, paid to 11 men and one reserve. Registered players would be permitted to help other clubs within a reasonable distance of their residence or work, with the consent of their own clubs. Minimum admission was fixed at one shilling, though clubs might offer reduced prices to servicemen, women and boys. A restrictive 50-mile travel limit was lifted if the return journey was completed on the day of the game.

The London Combination, which had organised a first team tournament in World War One, was chafing at the lack of a competition, and announced that they would start a regional competition at the end of October. The League was still tinkering with its own regional plans: while it tried to reach some conclusion, the season was passing by, making plans still more difficult. Eventually, Sunderland decided it would be better to close down. Among the friendlies on 30 September was a match that Leeds won 3–1 at Derby on a hard pitch which had been too closely mown by the Derby players themselves. Leeds needed to display some 'pretty footwork' to cope with the conditions. Finally, on 2 October the League came up with its plan for regional competition to start on 21 October, but Aston Villa, Sunderland, Derby, Exeter, Ipswich and Gateshead all declined to take part.

Even those who eventually played were not entirely happy with the plan, with most of the objections coming from the London clubs, particularly those south of the river. The South 'B' League included Brentford, Fulham, Queen's Park Rangers and Chelsea, and they were paired with Bournemouth, Southampton, Brighton, Aldershot and Reading. In all there were eight groups as follows: South 'A' (London teams), South 'B' (South London and the south coast), South Western, Western, Midlands (Luton to Leicester), East Midland (Nottingham to Sheffield), North Western and North Eastern. The normal points rules applied but the plan did not include win/draw bonuses. The clubs were to share proceeds on a 50–50 basis. Players had to provide their own clothing coupons to buy playing kit – though sometimes supporters were invited to help them out.

London clubs reckoned they had been carved up for no good reason, but eventually agreed to join in, insisting on an additional sixteen-club competition based on two groups, reflecting pre-war divisional status. Nobody was going to be entirely satisfied, and it was after all at the clubs' insistence that the FA returned to competitions in the first place. There was an understandable feeling that smaller clubs were being coerced by the bigger, a situation which is not unfamiliar 50 years later.

A familiar pairing during the war was the representative game – often between FA teams and selections from services' centres. The first was at Aldershot, where the FA, with eight internationals, played a 'Camp and Town' side, with five Aldershot FC players and six cappped Army players from other clubs. The FA won 1–0 with a goal from Lester Finch, one of two amateurs in the side. There was a 10,000 crowd, which made rather a nonsense of the theory that big matches in sensitive areas were undesirable. Plainly, the public wanted them, and £364 was raised from gate receipts and a collection.

As for amateur soccer, within six weeks or so the teams had also regrouped, and London clubs were making a real effort to carry on their League competition.

Competitive soccer returned to Britain on 21 October 1939. Public reaction to the new Leagues was initially less than wildly enthusiastic, with gates scarcely larger than for the friendlies, and barely keeping takings above running costs, despite reductions in payments to the players. Comparative attendance figures for 1938–9 and 1939–40 show the trend.

| | DATE | ATTENDANCES | GAMES PLAYED |
|---|---|---|---|
| 1938 | 6 November | 685,000 | 44 |
| 1939 | 21 October | 170,000 | 41 |
| | 28 October | 130,000 | 41 |
| | 4 November | 101,000 | 41 |

International matches, pulling crowds of 28,000 and 17,000 at Cardiff and Wrexham respectively boosted crowds to 210,000 and 174,000 on the next two Saturdays, but there was a slump down to 119,000 by 9 December.

*Mass Observation*'s man in Blackburn, though he still did not find more than one spectator talking about the war, was very impressed by the first match of the new League – between Blackburn and Blackpool:

The football match was interesting from many points, the crowd was larger, there was plenty of conversation and the people seemed more animated and alive than at any previous match. Whether this was because the match was competitive as distinct from the friendlies or whether it was due to the fact that people are gradually accepting the war, I cannot say.

However, on 11 November, there was 'terrible football, a waste of time going. No interest either by the spectators or players, very poor crowd, less than a thousand'. On that sad note, his reports ended.

Curiously, the games produced a spate of goal-scoring: a total of 163 goals were scored on 21 October 1939, and 193 the following Saturday, compared with 140 on 6 November 1938. An early enthusiast told *Mass Observation*: 'Mighty good, this war football, one sees a great big lot of goals, and the players, well, they're all turned wizards, you see them and forgets all about points and refs.' And a QPR fan agreed: 'I think it's better, more enjoyable to watch. I have an idea they play the game for the game, not to prevent goals being scored.'

There were other possible reasons for this spate of goals being let in, of course; many players had enlisted, guests did not always fit in (or had to be specially accommodated), training was reduced and the 30 shillings a match reward was scarce incentive to overdo things. (Bryn Jones, Arsenal's record signing at £14,000, was forced by poverty to return to Wales, and most players who were not in various services, took other jobs.) Footballers eschewed the 50–50 ball; as one professional explained: 'I don't know whether you've noticed, when two players go for a ball, one always lets the other one have it.'

Most spectators go to football to see goals scored – particularly by the sides they support. Accommodating guests was probably easier then, when every player knew his job – as goalkeeper, full-back, half or forward, but plainly the quality of guest varied. However, other potential spectators were less easily satisfied. They said that the

*Arsenal played their home matches at White Hart Lane during the war. The crowd at the November 1940 game against Charlton is typical of the early years.*

players were obviously not giving of their best on the field (though most of them would deny this, the risk of injury with no other employment to go to must always have been at the back of their minds). Unfamiliar Leagues, which presented the likes of Tranmere thrashing Everton, did not stir imaginations. Favourite players were absent. As one fan commented: 'You can't follow the matches now. You don't know who's who.' That and the worry and confusion brought on by the war itself deeply unsettled the previous common experience of sport. There was increased work, war duties, the absence of young fans who had enlisted and the

fact that the weekend was a chance perhaps to see evacuated families; these were other cogent reasons for the fall in the number of spectators.

Yet the FA's low-key approach seems to have worked. They did not make the mistake of 1914–5 and try to continue as normal. Nobody appeared to be hostile to professional soccer carrying on at a local level apart from some authorities, who objected for alleged safety reasons. International matches between the home countries continued to be astonishingly well supported, though still putting out teams of variable strengths. Soccer was a welcome bonus for those who wanted it – not least the players who later travelled in hazardous circumstances to away matches.

The Players' Union, in November 1939, looked for an increase in pay to £2 per match plus a bonus scheme. The League turned the bid down because gates had not improved enough to justify more money, and it rejected win/draw bonuses on principle. It was a very unpleasant winter and fog caused postponements on 23 December. There was only one Regional League match played on 3 Feb: Plymouth beat Bristol City 10–3.

The rebellious London soccer teams for the moment got their way and the clubs, based on previous Divisional status, made up 'C' and 'D' Leagues. They eventually completed the earlier competition, with Arsenal running out as group 'A' champions. Group 'B', which mostly contained the reluctant out-of-London travellers, went to QPR. In the new Leagues, Tottenham took the senior title, and Crystal Palace the minor ('D'). Hardly surprisingly, Bournemouth and Boscombe and Norwich, languishing at the bottom of 'D', didn't think it worthwhile completing their programmes with a match against each other. The South Western group was won by Plymouth (with 36 points from 28 matches), the Midlands by Wolves (41 points) and the East Midland by Chesterfield, with two Nottingham clubs propping up the table. The Western was won by Stoke, from Liverpool and Everton, and the North Western by Bury.

The North Eastern was won handsomely by Huddersfield, and had Leeds actually played the last two of their scheduled matches, they would still not have caught them. With the coming of spring and the Leagues producing crucial results, crowds increased significantly. March saw an average of 170,000, with a maximum of 226,000 – double that of some of winter's darker days.

On 4 March, an extension to the season (to 8 June) was granted for a war Cup to take place. Bonuses were also introduced: £1 for a win and ten shillings for a draw. 'Guests' were banned from this competition, but the attempt to re-impose peace-time conditions caused difficulties. Many players refused to turn up for their old clubs – five appealed to the Management Committee to be allowed to play for teams near their service depots,

and others, in war work, said that their employers had refused to allow them to travel. In a complicated structure, the third division clubs were first involved. Then four of them progressed to the first round proper, which was played on a home-and-away basis, as was the second.

The third round, on 18 May, and the remaining rounds, reverted to straight knock-out, with replays if necessary. The entire competition, of 137 games (including replays and Final) was condensed into seven weeks. A fair crowd of 42,399 watched West Ham, with a goal from Sam Small, beat Blackburn Rovers. Both teams fielded only their own players. Presumably it was slightly easier to persuade COs and employers to let you off for an engagement at Wembley than for a run-of-the-mill Regional League match. A. V. Alexander, the First Lord of the Admiralty, presented the medals; among the crowd were survivors of the previous week's retreat from Dunkirk. They had been admitted free. The end of the first war-time season thus coincided with England's darkest hour.

International fixtures met with a popular response. Wales drew a 40,000 crowd to Wembley in April 1940 (they won 1–0, through a Bryn Jones goal), while 75,000 watched Scotland and England draw 1–1 at Hampden Park on 11 May. In a notable war-time innovation, the teams were initially partly regionally-based. England used 31 players in their first three matches – one of these was the Walthamstow amateur, Lewis, brought on at Cardiff as a substitute.

With internationals, other representative matches and guesting, some of the better known players were able to improve on their basic 30-bob a week. Tommy Lawton squeezed a game for Morton in January 1941, whilst on honeymoon,

RIGHT *The first War Cup Final, at Wembley, drew a crowd of 42,399. West Ham beat Blackburn Rovers 1–0 with a goal from Sam Small.*

*The winter of '39–40 was a hard one, but The Army and England were not discouraged at Selhurst Park. Harper of England challenges Don Welsh.*

and managed two games on Christmas Day 1940, the first for Everton in a 3–1 defeat by Liverpool in the morning, and then, in the afternoon, scoring twice in a 2–2 draw for Tranmere at Crewe. Len Shackleton had a similar experience at Christmas, playing for both Bradford teams (Park Avenue and City) at Leeds and Huddersfield respectively. Guesting was not universally popular (for one thing it rendered the skills of the pools punters virtually useless); however, it did bring big names to some unlikely places. Although the system was open to some abuse, clubs did have genuine difficulties in raising teams, and some were even known to appeal to the crowd to make up numbers on occasions.

The clubs themselves also joined the war effort. A typical example was Reading, which raised £315 17s 6d for the Red Cross with an England XI v an Army XI (the proximity of Aldershot was no doubt a help in this). The club ran 'fitness for service' PT sessions and, in a scheme devised by Stanley Rous, the FA Secretary, ran a youth soccer training day at the ground. In addition, the club provided 28 leather footballs to be used by the forces in France.

Soccer had retained a visible identity, despite being very much 'at the sharp end' at the beginning of the war. It would continue to have its problems, particularly from the London clubs, but the public taste for soccer – and, not least, the players' enjoyment in getting a game and a few extra bob – gave it total justification.

Another familiar feature of the sporting scene soon returned, albeit in a deeply amended form: the pools. As early as 20 September, E. Holland Hughes, Secretary of the Pools Promoters' Association, said that public demand and the desire of members to give employment to as many as possible had led them to decide to reintroduce them on 7 October. English and Scottish fixtures would be used where available, and supplemented as necessary with Irish League matches. This

apparently high-minded intention was a clear example of the links between commerce and sport, and was quite possibly a spur to organising a regularised and competitive soccer programme. Though they received no direct payments, the football authorities similarly believed that pools would restore interest in the game, thereby helping to increase attendances.

The first attempt to revive the pools foundered on the postal services' refusal to deal with the mail, despite strenuous lobbying by the Pools Promoters. Although some of the smaller pools used a network of agents, Littlewoods operated entirely by post. *Mass Observation* estimated that about half the adult population had been involved. The receipt of the weekly package, including two coupons – one to pass on to a friend – was a high point of the week for millions of working people. The coupons were accompanied with other leaflets, greetings, a return envelope and the current issue of *Littlewood Sports Log*.

The idea of the package was to make all the punters feel part of a happy, lucky family. Apart

BELOW *Whatever the early state of the crowd, the team benches were well-filled, early on!*

## LITTLEWOODS · VERNONS · COPES · SHERMANS
## SOCAPOOLS · BONDS · JERVIS · SCREEN
# UNITY POOL

**Matches JAN 10th** — IN ALL POOLS PUT 1—HOME 2—AWAY X—DRAW — POOL 1 **9** RESULTS — POOL 2 **3** DRAWS — POOL 3 **4** AWAYS

*If you wish to invest on ONLY ONE of Pools 1, 2, or 3 and need more columns, you may use the columns of the other pools provided you cross out the headings.*

*PERMUTATION ENTRIES and entries on plain paper cannot be accepted and ONLY ONE OFFICIAL UNITY POOL COUPON can be accepted from each Client. One Coupon only can be posted in one envelope.*

| | |
|---|---|
| Aldershot | West Ham |
| Brighton | Fulham |
| Chelsea | Arsenal |
| Clapton O. | Watford |
| Crystal P. | Brentford |
| Millwall | Charlton |
| Tottenham | Reading |
| Barnsley | Grimsby T. |
| Bolton W. | Chester |
| Bradford | Middlesbro |
| Bristol C. | Bourn'm'th |
| Burnley | Man. City |
| Bury | N. Brighton |
| Doncaster | Halifax T. |
| Everton | Blackburn |
| Gateshead | York C. |
| Hudd'field | Sheff. Utd. |
| North'pton | Walsall |
| Notts F. | Chest'field |
| Preston | Liverpool |
| Rochdale | Leeds Utd. |
| Sheff. Wed. | Bradford C. |
| Sunderland | Newcastle |
| Swansea | Cardiff C. |
| Tranmere | Southport |
| West Brom. | Stoke C. |
| Wrexham | Stockport |
| Airdrie | St. Mirren |
| Clyde | Hearts |
| Falkirk | Partick T. |
| Hibernian | T. Lanark |
| Morton | Dumbarton |
| Motherwell | Celtic |
| Queens P. | Hamilton |

**MINIMUM STAKE PER COLUMN 6d**

**IMPORTANT** Post your coupon NOT LATER THAN THURSDAY to ensure it reaching us in good time. Seal the envelope (2½d. stamp).

### IMPORTANT ANNOUNCEMENT

Owing to the reduction in our staff necessarily occasioned in present circumstances, we have had to make certain alterations in our Coupon, to enable us to cope with the work entailed. We feel sure that our Clients will readily appreciate the position.

ADDRESS YOUR ENVELOPE
F.P.P.A. UNITY POOL (Comp.)

## The EASY SIX
Min. Stake per col. **6d** — Max. Stake per col. **5/-**

| | |
|---|---|
| Millwall | Charlton |
| Notts F. | Chest'field |
| Swansea | Cardiff C. |
| Clyde | Hearts |
| Falkirk | Partick T. |
| Motherwell | Celtic |

**MIN STAKE PER COL 6d**

## 2D POINTS POOL
4 DIVIDENDS FORECAST ALL 40% 25% 20% 15% — 14 MATCHES

| | |
|---|---|
| Aldershot | West Ham |
| Chelsea | Arsenal |
| Millwall | Charlton |
| Tottenham | Reading |
| Bolton W. | Chester |
| Burnley | Man. City |
| Doncaster | Halifax T. |
| North'pton | Walsall |
| Notts F. | Chest'field |
| Swansea | Cardiff C. |
| West Brom. | Stoke C. |
| Clyde | Hearts |
| Falkirk | Partick T. |
| Motherwell | Celtic |

YOU MUST SIGN YOUR NAME IN BLOCK LETTERS ON THE BACK OF YOUR ENVELOPE BEFORE POSTING

Credit only — 2d 2d 2d 2d 2d — 12 attempts 2/- — **22** – D2

**RULES and CONDITIONS** appear in The Leader, R.A.F. Outlook, Sporting Life, or will be sent on application

I AGREE (if this Coupon is accepted by you) to abide by your Rules and Conditions and PROMISE to remit NEXT WEEK total staked on this coupon (I am not under 21).

Name ............... BLOCK LETTERS
Address ...............
Town ...............
I enclose P.O. value £ : : No. ............... made payable to "UNITY POOL" and crossed for investments of 3rd JAN. (or ............... date)

*Amount invested on coupon must not be less than* 1

---

from football information, supplied by a gnome-like figure called 'The Little old man of the Wood', there were household hints and horoscopes which almost inevitably predicted that 'the Unexpected will materialise with full force'. However, the failure of millions of pools coupons to materialise on the doorsteps of Messrs. Littlewoods, Vernons, Copes, Shermans, Bonds, Jervis etc., was an unwelcome blow. After this rebuff from the GPO, the Pools Promoters agreed to join together in Unity Pools, which reached their clients through newspaper advertisements, and instructed the punters 'not to write in blotty ink'. Part of the takings were to go to war charities, though the charities had poor pickings at first. It was estimated that only 12% of the normal peace-time clients continued to 'invest' in the pools. Whereas a first dividend of £10,000 had been commonplace before the war, Unity's first three weeks produced dividends of £1,500, £750 and £1,073, falling to £250 in the first week of December. This was hardly surprising because the punters were unfamiliar with the regional system, and baffled by the constantly changing make-up of the teams and swapping of players which produced inconsistent form. This all destroyed what many believed to be their knowledgeable and skilled approach, based on ascertainable facts, and so reduced their chance of success. Not surprisingly, they decided that their money would be better spent elsewhere.

By January 1940, it looked as though the pools companies were facing ruin, unable to pay high enough dividends to attract the punter. By April, however, Unity Pools had clawed back to 33% of pre-war clients. Improved weather and greater familiarity with the new systems no doubt contributed to the upturn. The penny pools dividend was up to about £5,000, with a freak payment of £11,000 when the 'four aways' came up to odds of

LEFT *The* Unity Pool, *published in newspapers, started slowly, but picked up when punters got used to new fixture arrangements.*

44,000 – 1. Although there was without doubt a feeling that gambling, even on the pools, was frivolous and inappropriate at this time, there was a certain attraction to having a 'wee wager', as though it were hedging against borrowed time. The Pools Promoters had been made forever wary of the postal service, and increased their network of agencies so that even during postal strikes (as in the summer of 1988) they were never put under such pressure again.

Not only the Pools Promoters benefited from the new system. Newspapers, now pools-coupon distributors, increased their sales on pools days. The increased space given over to pools advice, however, could not hope to compensate for the severe cut back in sports coverage. The following comparison illustrates the point.

| PAPER | TOTAL NO. OF PAGES (SUN 7 OCT. 1938) | COL. INCHES ON SPORT | TOTAL NO. OF PAGES (SUN 5 OCT. 1939) | COL. INCHES ON SPORT |
|---|---|---|---|---|
| News of the World | 24 | 619 | 16 | 205 |
| Sunday Times | 32 | 419 | 18 | 386 |
| Sunday Express | 32 | 499 | 18 | 86 |
| Sunday Dispatch | 24 | 435 | 16 | 205 |
| Observer | 32 | 384 | 18 | 65 |
| People | 24 | 329 | 18 | 157 |
| Sunday Pictorial | 24 | 153 | 18 | 27 |
| Sunday Graphic | 32 | 157 | 18 | 9 |

This was at a time when the reorganisation of sport on a war-time basis had begun – soccer and rugby were being played, and horse racing was re-establishing itself. The News of the World and the Dispatch cut their sports service least. Yet there is another distinction: 'betting' sports did better than the others – even The Times started taking an interest in dog racing. There was an 80 per cent cut in coverage of non-betting sports – compared with an average 40 per cent reduction in newsprint.

The public's attitude to war news seems to have been fairly lukewarm. Although it often filled 90 per cent of the paper, 48 per cent of the population – according to Mass Observation – did not turn to it first. One suspects that the sports news might have been regarded as having greater credibility, and maybe relevance, in these early days of the war. The readers voiced their objections to the newspapers' policy, complaining that full details (scorers, team lists, etc.) were not given. It was widely felt that sports news could provide a diversion from the problems of war. It was a means of relaxation and also a way of maintaining a semblance of normality. There was plenty of war news on the radio as it was, and many people felt it was all too much.

The size of newspapers continued to dwindle, and along with it the sports coverage. For example, the Sunday Times was down to 12 pages with 73 column inches of sport by April 1940, and the Dispatch down to 12 pages with 121 column inches. The Daily Herald was at 4 to 5 columns of sport instead of 20 to 25, and The Times had three columns instead of 15 to 20. Moreover, 75 per cent of the Herald's sports news, and 61 per cent of The Times' was devoted to betting sports, dog and horse racing, pools advice and coupons. The public appeared to be getting used to their war-time papers, no longer missing their three or four pages of sport. One soccer fan's comment, when asked what he wanted, was: 'more war news, of course. There's much more to read, although it's pretty shocking.' A cricketer interviewed by Mass Observation agreed: 'War news must take preference. But I follow sports news just the same as I did before.'

Some papers introduced Diary columns – by 'Polaris' in the Star and 'Twelfth Man' in the Evening News – featuring odds bits of news, reminiscences of great personalities and great sporting events of the past. Cosgrave, the Star's sports editor, regarded these as doing 'the best to keep sport going by giving it as much publicity as we can', and thought that these reminiscences were 'the most likely to stir up interest'. It was implicit in this observation that there could be no great sporting events during the war.

'England has now begun the great Test Match with Germany', wrote Home Gordon portentously in his *Cricketer* leader, approving the view of Sussex captain Flt Lt A. J. Holmes that the Germans stood as little chance of winning 'as a snowball would in hell'. But the initial lack of action – with the teams, as it were, remaining in the pavilion – led to an increasing sense of unreality and frustration at seemingly unnecessary restrictions. As Novy acutely noted, the war was satisfying no one, least of all the bellicose. It was, he thought, being treated like one big sporting event in which 'one side brings down one of the other's aeroplanes, 15 love, then there is a retaliation, 15 all, and so on, into innumerable deuce games and sets stretching beyond the horizon.'

Many of the initial precautions began to appear unnecessary as the 'Phoney War' continued. Sport continued to re-emerge, although some authorities persisted in their over-zealous measures. Birmingham City, for example, were forbidden to play at home – although the city's dog racing continued, with thousands in attendance. The 'ban on Brum' was eventually lifted just before Easter 1940. As the local evening paper, which had led a campaign for the City's football fans, remarked: 'The Germans are foul and dirty fighters, but even they could hardly be expected to choose Saturday afternoon specially as the time, and the football ground of the Birmingham club as the locale, of their first manifestation of frightfulness against the civil population.'

The blackout which had been imposed at the start of the war had had an immediate effect on many sports. Complete and all-embracing, it had severely hit speedway racing, dog racing and even table-tennis, which experimented with phosphorescent balls under decreased lighting (another wartime innovation which has been developed in the present day, notably with odd-coloured cricket balls to suit TV and the night-time 'pyjama game' in Australia).

But by the late spring of 1940, the mood and tempo of the war had changed. It became evident that some of the precautions were not only unnecessary but even counter-productive. Cars forbidden to use their headlights had caused road deaths to double in September. Masked headlights were subsequently authorised. The first evacuation was a massive operation; one and a half million schoolchildren, plus teachers and mothers of under-fives moved officially, and probably another two million went unofficially. By January 1940, however, a million had returned home. The immediate clamp-down on sport was one of those emergency precautions which had to be revised, as soccer had proved. Other sports soon struggled back to some sort of organised competition.

Horse racing had stopped, and many courses were at once commandeered by the Government. Yet it restarted after a few weeks, with a first meeting at Newmarket on 17 October 1939, though necessarily a makeshift affair. Frank Harvey reported in the *Sunday Dispatch*:

For the past six weeks racing has been forgotten, except in those circles where nothing else matters. Stables occupied by famous racehorses have been emptied for other purposes; employees have had to turn their hands to sterner labour; large numbers of young thoroughbreds have been painlessly put to death; stagnation has reigned everywhere. On the whole, a very sorry business – but quite unavoidable, since none could say when, or under what circumstances, racing would be resumed again. Nevertheless, the Jockey Club, by virtue of its standing, has managed to outline a programme of fixtures which will be carried through while

RIGHT *The Derby was moved to Newmarket in June 1940. Unlike other wartime events, it retained its full status. The punters were there in force.*

*Pont L'Eveque (S. Wragg up) leading the way to victory in the 1940 Derby, the first in WWII held at Newmarket.*

conditions are favourable, and so it comes to pass that racegoers can foregather at Newmarket next Wednesday after their long spell of idleness. The joyful reunion takes place on the July course.

Newmarket, Thirsk, Newbury, Manchester, Wetherby, Gatwick, Plumpton and Windsor were among the earlier courses used. There were only about four meetings a week, as this was the minimum amount that it was economic to run. It was felt by punters and the course authorities that this was barely sufficient and, with meetings often starting as early as noon, even the courses nearest to London – Gatwick and Windsor – were not easy to reach in time.

As with soccer, the professionals were involved in financial worries, as owners suspended their

season's contract with their jockeys. Leading riders lost their large retainers, but there were some hopes that old associations would continue despite the circumstances.

The jockeys responded in different ways to the war: Charlie Smirke took to the jumps during flat racing's close season, while some spent the winter months 'digging for victory'. Leading riders like Sean Magee, Danny Morgan, George Archibald and Fred Rickaby were granted enough leave to do a fair amount of riding; Willie Rickaby was in the RAF and Tommy Hawcroft, sensibly enough, was in the Royal Veterinary Corps.

Before the war, racing had been a highly sociable event, with champagne and cigars much in evidence, but now the atmosphere was much more serious. In fact, betting was the crucial factor in the continuation of racing at all. Even without the Tote at first – and off-course cash betting was then illegal – the punters turned up, and bet with the bookmakers. Indeed the crowds rivalled those of peacetime, much to the surprise of those who put up small prizes expecting low attendances. One of the leading bookmakers at Newmarket commented that he had been taking as much as £1,000 a race in bets, and he even found himself a loser at times.

Hardest hit, particularly by the reduced prize-money, were the small owner-breeders. They gained the gratitude of the general racing world, however, for it was they who maintained the British thoroughbred through war-time. An owner who bought his yearlings at the sales instead of breeding them himself could liquidate his interests much more easily than the owner-breeder. Horses in training could either be sold or turned out in a paddock, but the owner-breeder had little option but to carry on.

The main problem, however, was the small prizes. One two-day meeting at Wetherby offered maximum prize money of £58 to the winner. With prizes at this level the small owner was likely to be driven out of the game. The jockeys too, whose remuneration was based on the value of the prize to be won, found themselves in straitened circumstances. Even big races were affected: the prize for 1940's Grand National was worth only £4,150 to the winner, whereas the previous year's winner had received £7,384 10s. The owner of the

*An idyllic Gatwick Racecourse, closed for ever for Service purposes during the war. Now it speeds jets, not horses.*

winner, Bogskar, was Lord Stalbridge, whose chagrin at reduced prize money might have been lessened by the winning price, 25–1. This was to be the last war-time National, as Aintree was soon requisitioned for the war effort.

At the top end of the market, however, breeders continued to fare remarkably well. While smaller breeders might be obliged to reduce stud fees, the larger and richer ones, possibly comforted by the slow start to the war, and the belief that, when it livened up, it would be quickly won, continued to pay high breeding prices. The Aga Khan's un-beaten triple classic winner, Bahram, was available to stand for 500 guineas; his Blue Peter and Polaris were fully booked up at 400 guineas for 1940.

The *Observer*'s special correspondent noted with some pride that:

> It is now practically certain that every import-ant owner-breeder will not be influenced in any degree by war-time conditions. I do not suppose that there is another country in the world of which that could be said in similar circum-stances. It is such things which go to prove the stability of the country and its inhabitants.

The fact that the Lincoln and the National were run before huge crowds, unlimited by police restrictions, as well as the continuing strength of the breeding market and the popularity of betting meant that racing could continue something like normal.

Racecourses – large, open areas of flattish land, not then used for farming purposes – naturally did not escape the attention of the authorities. After they had been taken over, many did not re-open after the war. In all, 16 closed for good including Aldershot, Bridgnorth, Derby, Totnes and Gat-wick. Aintree, home of the Grand National, did of course return to host the world's greatest steeple-chase after the war, although its future has never been quite certain since then.

Cricket, at the top level, dithered. By the time it came to the season of 1940, the cricket authorities had had several months to improvise or, indeed, to create a newly structured organisation. Few, in this war, believed that sporting activity up to a certain level was improper. R. C. Robertson-Glasgow, a wit but a man of deep sensitivity, wrote that 'there was no reason for wearing sackcloth and ashes in advance'.

However, notions of competition were rejected. Counties of the south – Sussex, Essex and Middle-sex (Surrey's ground had been taken over, but perhaps they might have played at Guildford) – wanted a regional competition at weekends includ-ing playing on Sundays. Obviously, nothing like a full County championship, on the pre-war basis, could take place. Players could not be released from their other duties, civilian or military, for anything like a three-day period, but the author-ities' view was not very flexible. The administra-tors were of an older generation, conservative and prone to 'war puritanism'. The County Cham-pionship itself – of three-day matches – had scarcely been retaining interest before the war. (Home Gordon had written of a 'melancholy half-hearted apathy' in the last matches). Two-day matches had been tried in 1919 and abandoned as a disaster.

County cricket clubs were, in any case, on the horns of a dilemma: their first responsibility was to their members, and only secondly to the public. The three-day game was considered to be the purest form of cricket, and the only true training ground for great players. However entertaining it might be, the shorter game could never be proper first-class cricket.

So no attempt was made to set up regional one- or two-day matches based on the existing first-class counties, nor competitions involving the services and regional teams, perhaps with guest

RIGHT *The Aga Khan's triple-classic winner, Bahram, had a stud fee of 500 guineas. He sired the very successful Big Game.*

players as had happened in soccer.

Instead they decided to improvise matches. Almost all of them were one-day games, played whenever and wherever possible. Lord's devised a programme of 19 matches, with more to follow, by 12 April. Under this ad hoc system it was not surprising that much of the motivation came from personal (and private) enterprise, especially in the south.

The counties generally failed to respond to the challenges to organise themselves. R. C. Robertson-Glasgow pointed out, somewhat cattily, that 'as a study in finance, even satire, it is interesting to note that a few counties have actually gained through the absence of cricket. Expenses have dropped to a minimum, and a large number of subscriptions have been received'.

Essex, Sussex and Kent were all labelled Defence Areas, which meant that teams were stopped from travelling into restricted parts and so they gave what encouragement they could to club cricket in their areas. Northamptonshire, Leicestershire and Nottinghamshire arranged a handful of matches around the East Midlands. Surrey played local club sides. Worcestershire played Warwickshire on 5 August in a very friendly match with free admission but a heavily-plugged invitation to contribute to the Worcester Fighter Club.

Two teams dominated southern cricket in the war: London Counties and the British Empire XI. Both teams had their first games on 5 May 1940; the Empire XI was the brainchild of 19-year-old Desmond Donnelly, while London Counties, formed by C. J. E. Jones of Forest Hill, was a team of professionals 'with a hint of syndicalism about them'. The teams echoed the missionary days of Victorian cricket, when the game was spread round the country and eventually the world, with tours to Australia by pros who needed a reliable living. However, the main aim of Jones and his men was to raise money for war charities.

The youthful Donnelly, who later became an MP of various political shades, before his tragic death, was immensely persuasive and managed to attract famous players like R. E. S. Wyatt to his side. Before the first match he phoned Reg Hayter, then a junior Press Association reporter, to ask if he could help provide some cricketers for his team. Hayter managed a couple, including himself, and thought the idea might be worth a paragraph for publicity. But what to call the team? Mr D. Donnelly's XI was scarcely inspirational and so the magnificent title of the British Empire XI emerged. Donnelly believed that this team would, eventually, help knit the soldiers and sportsmen of the colonies and dominions together, even if they were thin on the ground at the time. His greatest aquisition was C. B. Clarke, the West Indian tourist of the previous summer.

As a gimmick, the XI's first match, against Rosslyn Park in aid of the Red Cross, was played for a side-stake of a barrel of beer. Hayter himself was at the wicket with Hugh Bartlett when the barrel was duly won by six wickets for the Empire XI. The team played on an amateur basis, and was a mixture of club and first-class cricketers. A strong Cambridge University XI trounced them by an innings later that summer despite a second-innings score of 139 by Norman Yardley. He was accompanied in this stand with a fighting 56 from W. M. F. Bebbington, recently invalided out from the army (he had previously played for Darjeeling). Despite his now having only one lung, according to Hayter, he became the team's regular wicketkeeper. He enjoyed a particularly purple spell from mid-August to the end of September, scoring 700 runs with an average of nearly 80.

One unexpected discovery was the Chingford club opening batsman L. F. Parslow, who had previously only reached the heights of Essex Club and Ground. He netted 900 runs at an average of 45 and received great praise from *Wisden* for his technique, immaculate style and ability to cope with first-class bowling, despite having learned his game mostly through practice with friends and reading a book on batsmanship by C. B. Fry. His temperament, while making a century against London Counties before a huge crowd at Lord's, was greatly appreciated.

An attraction of these games was to see famous players in relatively out-of-the-way places like Tunbridge Wells, Gravesend and Slough. The club teams were sometimes also boosted by famous names, for example Dulwich Hamlet included L. J. Todd of Kent for their game against London Counties.

The Empire XI provided high-class opposition. Denis Compton played a couple of times for them, as did Ken Farnes, Eddie Ingram from Ireland, who topped the bowling averages at 7.10 (but with only a quarter of the wickets of West Indian Bertie Clarke at 10.74), Eddie Watts, Ray Smith from Essex, Conradi and Bridger from Cambridge. The most frequent captain was Hugh Bartlett, the massive Sussex hitter, who was often a great source of inspiration. Under his direction, attractive batting and crafty spin were the norm. Another captain was the Northamptonshire skipper, R. P. Nelson, who topped the batting averages

*Denis Compton, getting the ball away to leg, was an immense attraction during the war, in this country at first, and later in India.*

at 49.83. Previously he had transformed his county's fortunes in just one season. Sadly, he was killed by a bomb in the early autumn.

C. J. E. Jones had organised benefit matches for professionals like Larwood, Ames and Woolley before the war and so he was well acquainted with many of them. He was thus quick to realise the difficulties that the breakdown of organised county cricket would cause them. The players had been used to a relatively high standard of living; but, given their social and educational backgrounds many struggled to gain any special status in the Services and so began to feel the pinch fairly quickly.

In February 1940 Jones, Hobbs, Woolley and Hendren met to discuss the forthcoming season. The players were alarmed at the authorities' reluctance to set up an organised structure and felt that their livelihood was in danger and that their skills could waste away. To prevent this from happening they decided to form their own club, London Counties, with Jack Hobbs as president. It was agreed that gate receipts should be given to the cricketers – who, for their own part, insisted that a proportion of this should go to charity. These were craftsmen cricketers; they argued that all matches should be played with complete commitment: runs were not to be given away by bowlers and slack fielding would not be tolerated. Only if the cricket was played properly would people be interested in watching it regularly.

They were a very successful team, winning 23 of their 26 fixtures and drawing two. Two of their leading players were Arthur Fagg and Jack Durston, the youngest and oldest in the side. Fagg had not been accepted by the Army, because of the effects of rheumatic fever that he had contracted on the MCC tour to Australia four years earlier. Despite this he scored 1,098 runs (average 57.36), usually in rapid time, before leaving to join the RAF. The side also offered the possibility of some tail-end turbulence from three of the game's biggest hitters, Jim Smith, Arthur Wellard and

Watt of Kent. Durston, then aged 46, was no longer the tearaway who had played against Australia in 1921. He allied length and spin in a manner which most club players found too much for them and took 61 wickets at 9.09. The team rotated the captaincy, often giving it to a player with local connections.

The highlights of the season in the south were the two matches between the London Counties and the British Empire XI at Lords. The first match on 13 July attracted 8,000 spectators and over £121 was raised for the Red Cross. However, it turned out to be disappointingly one-sided. The Counties, batting first, scored 259, with Hulme (78) top scorer. But, despite 54 from Parslow, Durston destroyed the middle order, including Denis Compton for one, and so the Counties won by 104 runs.

The second match resulted in the London Counties' only defeat of the season. The Empire XI batted first, and all the batsmen made something of a contribution in a total of 308 for 5 declared. Fittingly, Parslow made his first century at Lord's, Denis Compton made 60, and J. G. W. Davies of Kent added a crashing 51 not out. Frank Woolley, at 53, had a good game, picking up the wicket of Compton and scoring 38. But the Counties side never settled into the big innings needed. Denis Compton's left-arm tweakers brought him 6 for 81 as the Counties folded for 255. 10,326 paid at the gates, with receipts of £258; and a collection for the Red Cross and the Cricketers' Friendly Society gathered £145.

Eight thousand gathered at Lord's on the next Saturday for another run feast in which Sir Pelham Warner's XI beat a Club Cricket Conference team by three wickets, with Parslow among the runs again for the Clubs; but Denis Compton's galvanic 101 for Warner's XI was enough to ensure victory, although it was his brother, Leslie, who finished the job. Five days later, the brothers were at Lord's again. Denis played for Warner's team, scoring 73, and Leslie joined a West Indies

XI, which included Martindale, Constantine and Clarke. This range of talent was not enough to prevent Warner's side from winning by 117 runs.

It was a splendid cricketing summer. Many commented ironically on how sad it was that the war had disrupted it so badly for, by now, the 'Phoney War' had become real enough. In the summer of 1940, Germany conquered Holland and Belgium. The French collapsed in May. Chamberlain resigned, and was succeeded by Churchill, offering 'blood, toil, tears and sweat' and the promise of 'victory at all costs, victory in spite of all terror; victory, however long and hard the road may be'. But first Dunkirk had to be evacuated,

*The evacuation of Allied troops at Dunkirk was quite miraculous. Some wondered if sport was fitting in the circumstances, but survivors attended the Cup Final.*

enabling a million men, two-thirds of them British, to fight again. Italy entered the war and Hitler more or less offered peace in mid-July, but there was no mood to accept this. Sir Home Gordon was, as ever, ready with a sporting metaphor: Hitler 'has captured the first two wickets with his express grubs'. However, he averred 'our best bats have still to go in'. After the heavy losses of men and equipment before and during Dunkirk, thoughts of a gallant last-wicket stand might have seemed more appropriate. And that, indeed, was the case from July 1940 as the Battle of Britain was waged in the skies. At the crucial time the *Luftwaffe* changed its emphasis from attacking the airfields to bombing the cities, in revenge for RAF attacks on German cities. This took the pressure off the airfields and prevented the Germans from gaining air superiority. In October plans for the invasion of Britain were postponed.

Other cricket, of course, also took place. The MCC played no matches at Lord's, but had an extensive fixture list against the public schools, the nursery of post-war amateurs. Some of these matches had to be cancelled because the schools concerned were evacuated. Difficulties in travelling often hampered potential fixtures even when a decent ground and good wickets were provided, as when the Duke of Marlborough gave Malvern the use of the lovely ground at Blenheim Palace; G. H. Chesterton, later of Worcestershire, bowled well for them. Bristol Grammar and Clifton both had their seasons shortened when enemy action forced them to break up early for summer. H. A. Pawson, the Winchester captain, was the batsman of the year, but a young T. E. Bailey made an appearance in *Wisden*, scoring 33 and taking two wickets for Dulwich College in a six-wicket victory at Bedford. The figures only for this game appeared in *Wisden* because of the difficult circumstances in which it was put together. The preface to the 78th, 1941, edition explains the problem:

*One umpire's decision not to be questioned. The mower seems to have run out of petrol!*

*"Private Johnson—About-turn!"*

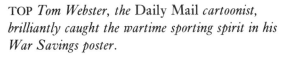

TOP *Tom Webster, the* Daily Mail *cartoonist, brilliantly caught the wartime sporting spirit in his War Savings poster.*

ABOVE *Hugh Bartlett, who captained the British Empire XI and won the DFC at Arnhem.*

RIGHT *Kent's Arthur Fagg, stalwart of London Counties.*

First, the publishers' premises were completely destroyed by enemy action at the end of 1940, and a large part of the editorial material being prepared for the printers was lost. Fortunately most of this was duplicated, but a small amount of interesting matter disappeared irretrievably. After this experience, additional precautions were taken, and so when a further supply of editorial was charred beyond recognition in the printer's office safe, it could be replaced, although the recompilation took some time. As a further blow the Public Schools section, entrusted to the post on the afternoon of the worst raid of the spring, did not reach its destination, and, while the scores and reports could be duplicated, the article on Public School Cricket could not be re-written, all the author's notes having been destroyed at another place at the same time. That is the explanation of the four advertisement pages [for various Wisden products] appearing so oddly on pages 185 to 188.

There were some significant social changes in the 1941 *Wisden*. Previously, all amateurs' names had been prefixed by 'Mr', or a military rank, or occasionally 'Rev', while the professionals were prefixed only by their initials (earlier, they did not qualify even for that). Now players were listed by their rank, whatever it was, if they were servicemen or with their initials if they were not. With such men as W. J. Edrich, H. Verity, L. E. G. Ames and H. S. Squires in the officer ranks the change was not only understandable, but probably even necessary. It reflected the improved status of the professional since the end of the First World War, and the development of a more egalitarian age. Also, for the first time, Northern and Midland League cricket reports were included.

Astonishingly, the Lancashire League decided to cancel their professionals' contracts. Without the flamboyance of the 'star' to attract them, attendances dwindled to a fraction of their usual levels.

The Birmingham League, after much discussion, decided to carry on more or less as usual with both professionals and amateurs playing. Old Hill won the title by one point from West Bromwich Dartmouth. They started in remarkable style, with Eric Hollies, the Warwickshire leg-spinner, taking all ten of Mitchell's and Butler's wickets for 21, on the first day of the season. He finished top of the bowling averages with 99 wickets at 9.91. Eight years later he wrote himself into history as the man who bowled Bradman for a duck in his final test at the Oval. R. E. S. Wyatt, who played for Moseley, topped the batting list with an average of 64.50, although W. E. Merritt, the New Zealand and Northamptonshire all-rounder, was the League's top scorer, with 878 runs, and he bagged 80 wickets as well. The most remarkable innings of the season came from Tom Goddard, the Gloucestershire off-spinner not normally noted for over-taxing the scorers, with a first-class average of about nine, who battered the long-suffering Smethwick for 140 in an hour and a half, with 11 sixes and nine fours.

The Yorkshire county side was involved in just three matches, and only one under their own name, against the Bradford League. The League were lifted by 100 from Constantine in an hour before he was caught by Captain Herbert Sutcliffe off the bowling of Sergeant-Instructor Len Hutton. Yorkshire, despite 127 from Sutcliffe, were content to let the game end in a draw. Seven thousand watched the match and receipts totalled £300 with a collection raising a further £80 for the Red Cross. The strength of the League's cricket was indicated by the fact that they picked a team almost entirely of Yorkshiremen, and still had the better of the match.

Eddie Paynter, lured over the Pennines, was in fact the most consistent bat in the Bradford League with 1,040 runs at 74.28, followed by Wilfred Barber, a Yorkshireman who scored a century for Brighouse in 36 minutes and passed all his 'collections' over to the Red Cross. The top all-

LEFT *The cover of the slim-line* Wisden *for 1941 (recording the previous summer's cricket). At the height of the Blitz, its contents just escaped German bombers' attentions.*

BELOW *Strong club teams, sometimes bolstered with guests, were put out to play visiting tourists. Slough v London Counties, 1940.*

rounder was George Pope of Derbyshire, with 88 wickets and 641 runs, overshadowing even Constantine, who averaged 30.50 with the bat and took 76 wickets. Constantine's team, Windhill, won the Division 'A' title, and Pope's side, Lidget Green, won the 'B'.

At the humblest end of the cricketing scale clubs struggled to survive as conscription and war-work bit deeply into their resources. The number of clubs operating fell and there was a corresponding decline in playing standards, with lads and greybeards being pressed into service, trying to make up in enthusiasm what they lacked in skill. The spirit of the players can best be summed up by a notice pinned to the gates of a leading south coast ground which had been slightly bomb-damaged:

> Local cricketers are as pleased as you. Each peardrop which fell on this ground saved lives and property. We shall carry on. Nothing which falls from the skies will deter us, except RAIN.

With the exception of soccer, national (not to mention international) sport appeared to be out of the question in the early days of the war. As mentioned earlier, the blackout put paid to events which needed artificial lighting on a large scale, and those sports which required large indoor spaces were subject to the demands of civil defence units and, later, light engineering works. Personal recreation and occasional charity events became the order of the day. The less highly-organised and essentially non-professional games, such as angling or bowls, were least affected, although the social life of local clubs was hard-hit as rationing came into effect. Sports clubs could rarely persuade their local Food Office that they were worthy recipients of a food allowance.

Petrol rationing put paid to distant fixtures, and many clubs decided to give up some of their time and equipment to allow for service practices, which meant restricting the time available for the members to use the facilities. Yet many clubs managed to adapt to the problems caused by war.

The novelty sport, roller speedway, disappeared for ever from these shores; and baseball, with little current following in Britain, was wiped out until the GIs revived it later. Motor cycle speedway racing was an early and major casualty. War broke out immediately before the World Championships were due to take place at Wembley and so the event was cancelled. Some of the colonial stars hurried home as fast as they could. Ronnie Greene of Wimbledon hit on the notion of encouraging the remainder to become dispatch riders, for which he was awarded an MBE. Others, like Tommy Combs and Bluey Wilkinson, went into mechanical trades. Occasional meetings at Belle Vue, Manchester were all that the rest of the war had to offer, because it was believed that afternoon racing at a competitive level would not be an economic venture.

Ice hockey drifted into a decline, from which it has never entirely recovered, despite Canadian service matches, particularly in the far north and south, later in the war. Young British players drafted into the teams, like Harsaut, Ridley, Dunkelman and Eves, failed to attract the crowds. In any case, it became increasingly difficult to bring players together for practices and matches. Administrative problems abounded, as when Bunny Aherne tried to take a Wembley team to Belfast. The trip foundered on a five-shilling pass: 'It was like trying to get them into Berlin'. But ice skating remained very popular, where it was available. After a regular Wembley match between the Lions and Greyhounds, which attracted 5,000 spectators in November 1939, there was an open session on the rink. A form of tennis on ice called 'ten-ice' was tried, but it did not catch on.

Wembley, the site of many of these experiments, certainly worked hard to promote sports. It was, it announced in an international football programme, 'doing everything possible to carry on and to maintain its position as the Sports Centre of the British Empire. Both at this Stadium and at the Empire Pool and Sports Arena we are doing our best to provide for sporting attractions which will help you forget for an hour or two the troubles and trials which beset us all at the present time'. The Wembley authorities spent £300 blacking out the glass roof in order to hold night-time events.

It appeared at first that snooker and billiards had remained untouched by the war, but this proved illusory. At Thurston Hall the audience fell to about a third of the pre-war average. Throughout the country many of the older spectators decided to stay inside during the blackout and so the halls struggled to survive. Spring 1940 saw Fred Davis playing his elder brother, Joe, for the World Championship at Thurston's. On the last evening, they were level at 36 frames all. Joe took the final one with a century break to keep the title. The Duke of Roxburghe made the presentations. Next October, Thurston's received a direct hit, destroying not only the Hall itself but an irreplaceable collection of billiards antiques which had been on loan for an exhibition. (Those who had hidden and buried their treasures were proven wise in the event).

Competitive lawn tennis effectively folded after a match between the Amateurs and the Professionals. The Lawn Tennis Association sent its records to the country and its players to the services. Tinkler and Wilde joined the artillery, Shayes and C. M. Jones the RAF and Lee was in the Pay Corps. Many women players had great difficulty in returning from America. There was a barrage balloon centre at Queen's Club, and people were quartered there, but some tennis was still possible. Many clubs opened their doors to servicemen on leave. At first Wimbledon became an Air Raid Precaution (ARP) and civil defence centre. A small farm sprang up in the car parks to grow crops and there was grazing for animals, but the sacred courts were spared. The men's dressing rooms were not so fortunate – a hole was knocked in the wall to allow stretchers to be passed quickly through.

So, although play was still possible at Wimble-

don, it was non-competitive and sporadic. It was often difficult to find an opponent of similar ability who was available at the right time. However, there were frequent exhibition games played for good causes, including one on 20 August 1941, in aid of the Chinese who were seen as allies in a common struggle. Among the players was Kenneth Lo, later to achieve wider fame as a restaurateur and instructor-chef. Professionals, who were struggling to make ends meet, were given blunt advice by E. A. Avery, a leading player: 'They will have to get jobs. Let's hope as few as possible will get killed and that they will all be ready to put things in order when war ends'.

Golf was similarly affected: the links themselves were obviously prime areas for military attention, as were the club houses. Although some golfers had to change in the caddy hut, it was noted that there was actually considerably less grumbling than usual. Not all golfers accepted the full consequences of the exigencies of war and they expected standards of dress and behaviour to be rigorously maintained. Yet club treasurers could not afford to be too particular, anxious as they were to balance the books and pay professionals and caddies despite a diminishing number of regular players. The sport remained expensive; a round for two could cost almost as much as the 30 shillings earned by a professional footballer.

Somehow one club managed to by-pass wartime stringencies and, in August 1941, could still offer the following lunch menu:

Windsor soup

Escalopes and spaghetti
Roast duck
Roast Lamb
New potatoes
French beans

A choice of four sweets

Cheese

However, Novy's dismissal of golf as 'a useful

refuge for our upper classes' was less true than ever thanks to the activities of professionals like Henry Cotton, the Open Champion in 1934 and 1937 (and again in 1948). As with cricket, the war accelerated the trend of lowering the barriers between professionals – who had previously been denied entrance to the club-house – and amateurs. None did more to raise the status of the golf professional than Cotton, who, in the worst part of the year for golf, plunged into raising funds for war charities: £625 was collected for the Red Cross during a match between him and Richard Barton against the amateur brothers A. L. and H. G. Bentley at Hesketh in November 1939. By the end of the year he had raised £3,000 for the Red Cross through games involving the Ryder Cup team and against top women golfers like Pam Barton and Wanda Morgan, who played from their own tees and received six shots on handicaps.

Many clubs suffered from a shortage of members, or the loss of certain key figures in their organisation. Wartime policies differed greatly: some let troops in at half price, while others preserved a distinction between men and officers. One club, Gosforth, Bridle Path, was so pleased with the filling in of a bomb cavity at its course, that it allowed a free round of golf to all serving officers in perpetuity. This still operates today.

On the outbreak of war it was expected that rugby would not be played for the duration because it was thought that the sport appealed largely to those of a war-like temperament. But on 28 October a large crowd gathered at the Old Deer Park in London showing that there was public demand for the game. Yet there were problems, as the clubs came into conflict with the game's establishment. This was a not untypical situation in many sports at the time. J. P. Jordan wrote:

> Many London rugby clubs who have opened their grounds and have been keeping the game alive are now faced with the prospect of having to close them down through financial reasons, following the unofficial hint that they cannot look to the Rugby Union for help. But it is difficult to see what the RU can do to help. There are over 1,000 clubs in England in

*Henry Cotton (*RIGHT *in uniform,* FAR RIGHT *in golfing gear), already twice Open champion, set about raising money for charities with great success.*

BELOW *Golf could provide a pleasant summer afternoon's diversion in 1940; amateurs and pros joined forces on the 16th at North Middlesex.*

membership. To make up the possible losses of even a tenth would drain the Union's resources and they do not exist for that purpose.

It was left up to the players, the clubs, the universities, the hospitals and the public schools, as well as benefactors like Major Stanley, to sort these matters out for themselves. However, the Union kept a watchful eye over the game, ready to punish any misdemeanours, and continued in its role as the sport's administrator.

Improvisation and private enterprise were the watchwords as fixture lists were scrapped and hurriedly revised. An unofficial Varsity match was so successful that it was planned to hold a return game at Oxford. Arthur Cornish and Wilf Wooller organised midweek games at Cardiff Arms Park for the Lady Plymouth Troops Comfort Fund.

A prime game was at Richmond in December 1939, a semi-international, when 7,000 saw England and Wales beat Scotland and Ireland 17–3, with a brilliant try by Obolensky, the Russian prince who had scored twice against the All-Blacks in his first match for England in 1936. In March 1940 he became the first rugby international to lose his life in the war after a flying accident. Schools' rugby flourished, with many taking on local Service sides in place of planned fixtures. Rugby School played Bedford for the first time ever (curious for such near neighbours).

BELOW *Wartime Varsity Rugby matches were successful, though Blues were not awarded. Cambridge's Newton-Thompson sets up Steeds.*

RIGHT *The dashing Russian, Prince Obolensky (in stripes) of Oxford, Rosslyn Park and England, was the first Rugby international to lose his life in the war.*

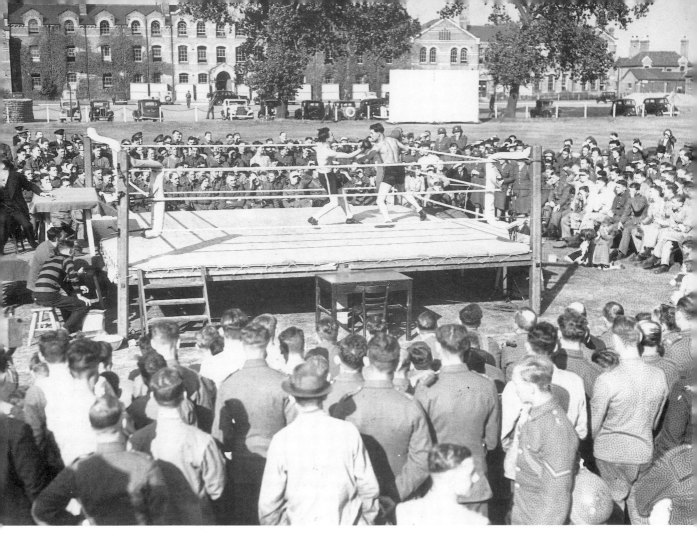

*Boxing exhibitions for the troops were often in the open air. At a barracks 'somewhere in England', Jock McAvoy fights Jack Hyams.*

However, there was a major problem: what to do about the Rugby League? The League (originally known as the Northern Union) had broken away from the ruling body on 29 August 1895 in protest against the Union's refusal to allow them to compensate players who took time off work to play rugby. It was far from being an outright professional sport – there remained a proviso that players must have some other outside employment. But the Rugby Union shunned the new code, forcing the Northern Union to make the sport much more attractive to the spectator. So, in 1906, they reduced the number of players per side from 15 to 13; next year, they allowed a player tackled in possession to regain his feet, and bring the ball into play by dropping it on the ground. This meant that a very different game had been

created. The Union's reply was to ban any players who had any dealings whatsoever with Rugby League, amateur or professional.

However, during the First World War, there had been a compromise, and so it was perhaps inevitable that the two codes would again come together in some small way, despite the opposition of those who felt they would be tainted by association with League players. So, on 12 November 1939 the Rugby Union allowed League players in the Forces to take part in matches between affiliated clubs and Services teams for the duration of the War. The Welsh and Scottish RUs reluctantly followed suit; the Welsh were particularly worried that their own members might set up a professional 15-a-side competition if attempts to stop lucrative club matches succeeded.

Rugby League had its own problems at first; it followed the now regular sporting custom of organisating matches in favour of the Red Cross, but the Yorkshire and Lancashire divisions decided to pay their players only £1 a match, instead of the £6 a week to which they had been accustomed. They naturally objected, and went into their games in a very half-hearted manner. The *Daily Worker* commented that what they served up was 'tea-party football'.

The only sport to do relatively well out of the start of the war was greyhound racing. Although a number of puppies were put down in the early days, in the belief that they would never earn their keep, it soon became obvious that afternoon meetings in the big conurbations were very popular among the night workers, who were the largest group of spectators. There were also servicemen on leave to be catered for and others still unemployed. Betting at the tracks held up well, with a belief that fewer punters were putting up rather more apiece. There was an estimate by *Mass Observation* that some 22 million dog-racegoers had passed through the turnstiles by the end of 1939; many of course had staged repeat journeys, and there were far more tracks about than nowadays. The size of the crowds became a worry, and because of this the Greyhound Racing Association abandoned its Oaks and made its Derby an all-ticket event at much less than actual capacity. An all-ticket approach might have been helpful to a number of sports, since one reason given for not travelling to matches was that the potential spectator might come a long way, and with great difficulty, only to find himself locked out. But, given the general disruption, it might have been difficult to acquire the tickets in the first place.

Boxing was thrown into turmoil as the managers were once again at odds with the Board of Control.

The point at issue this time was the Board's failure to award a Lonsdale Belt to Eric Boon (the belt was customarily strapped round a new British champion and kept in perpetuity if he managed three successive title wins). Sydney Hulls, Jack Solomons and Harry Levene made a stand of principle. However, there was a commercial angle to their action because the rent for premises remained the same, even though crowds were limited.

The Board had also imposed a levy of 5 per cent on all takings, to finance their own operations, whether or not the promotion made a net profit. Some leading, crowd-pulling fighters were unwilling to put their titles – let alone their health – at risk for a smallish reward and so a number of unlicensed promotions followed, but the boxing public remained indifferent to such matters. Hulls arranged fights between professionals in the Services for the entertainment of troops and this proved to be a major success, which showed once more the 'enthusiastic flame a fight kindles in the hearts of all classes of society'.

The amateur minor sports picked up on a fairly ad hoc basis, in general following the style of Rugby Union. Players looked for games where they could find them, and clubs were forever in search of players. Festival-style hockey teams were formed and they advertised themselves as being available for matches. The redistribution of the population meant a strengthening of some out-of-town women's teams; for example, Northampton had to refuse membership to some applicants, so great was the demand to join the club.

Countryside sports were relatively unaffected: the grouse shooting in 1939 was particularly good before the call-up took away gamekeepers, and predators took their toll. But swimming (with many baths closed), shooting (with most firing-ranges confiscated and men called up) and athletics all languished. The Athletics Southern Counties called off a meeting because of the number of men in the Services. Many of the athletes became PT sergeants in the army. Some team road-racing continued, but otherwise there was very little athletics. However, since little money was involved this was not widely noticed.

A major social effect of the war was the increasing influence of women in sport, as elsewhere in society. The British people, by and large, had not wanted a war, but been presented with one. As a result, the country was inadequately prepared, not least for the continuance of sporting activities. However, events were put together during the war's first year with some inventiveness and flexibility. Continuation of sport was generally seen as a congenial relaxation and – not the least important – an example of British *sang froid* which could only dispirit the enemy. But not everybody saw it that way.

# DISSENTING VOICES

'A WASTE of time, money and effort – but then [sports] always were. A spectacle which is a poor advertisement for the human race at the best of times becomes doubly so when Rome is burning.'

That was the view of a woman approached by *Mass Observation* early in 1942 about sport in general, and mass, organised sports in particular. Women's views on sport hardened during the war. These examples are typical of the attitude of many:

I have never considered the big sporting events of any importance and wish they would disappear for good and all.

No big sporting events should be allowed in wartime. Dog racing, horse racing and hunting should be abolished to prevent waste of food, waste of labour, waste of petrol and disruption of transport.

Boxing has always struck me as brutal and disgusting, and I can't even watch it in a newsreel. If boxing is necessary for military training and commandos, then it should be taught, but not practised in front of audiences.

These comments followed a speech in February 1942 by Sir Stafford Cripps, the new Leader of the House of Commons, when he urged a general tightening of belts. 'Personal extravagance is to be eliminated. All wastage, all unnecessary expenditure is to be ended,' reported the *Daily Mail*. 'Our motto,' he said, 'can neither be "Business as Usual" nor "Pleasure as Usual".' The tightening up of the war effort foreshadowed the closer control over dog racing, horse racing, boxing and similar activities.

There can be no doubt that the playing of sport for pleasure, as opposed to a specific physical fitness campaign, caused concern to many. Cricketers cavorting in the fields of Kent, as train-loads of Dunkirk survivors passed them by, might seem insensitive to say the least. Certainly some seamen reacted angrily when, in the wake of Dunkirk, the first wartime Cup final was being broadcast by the BBC at the same time as they were pulling bodies from the sea.

Despite this, there was not the widespread white-featherism of the First World War but, instead, there was a form of war puritanism which lingered in the minds of ordinary people and their governors. Sir John Anderson was a Presbyterian, Samuel Hoare a Quaker, John Simon and Lord Macmillan were sons of parsons; Ernest Brown was a Baptist preacher and Chamberlain a Unitarian preacher. These were not the type of men to encourage even the milder pleasures of the flesh at such a time.

Spectators became particular targets for attack

in a campaign whipped up by the press. They were accused of wasting transport capacity, whether by using petrol for their own cars or taking up seats on the trains, and it was believed that they were likely to be taking time off work and then going on a drinking binge afterwards, thus wasting manpower. They could not be seen to be improving their bodies or their souls like the sportsmen, indeed the opposite seemed to be the case. And yet, with diminished crowds, many events lost their appeal. One fan observed that 'the bigger the crowd, the better the football, for or against; with small crowds the games haven't got any go in

them'. Novy wrote, maybe with some prescience: 'It is not enough to be watching. It is important to be watching, yelling, booing, cheering and in some sports throwing things too.' Because of this rowdy behaviour crowds are often easy meat for authorities who think there is something wrong with society, but cannot trace exactly what.

Horse racing and dog racing provoked particular ire; the former perhaps because many conceived it as being a haven for the upper classes, the latter because of its lower-class connections. Both sports involved gambling, and war puritanism demanded that spare cash should be going to other

LEFT *Servicemen, off-duty and on leave, lost no time in making for vantage points to watch their favourites in action, despite the critics.*

BELOW *Daylight greyhound racing proved very popular. There were objections both to the gambling and to the temptation to take unofficial time off.*

and better causes. Furthermore, the animals consumed food that might be better used elsewhere. One correspondent added to the abolition of sport a range of other targets of popular prejudice inluding 'those West End hotel ideas, those Torquay funk-holes, all newspaper adverts and the thousand and one things that prevent us from a total war effort'.

In 1942 *Mass Observation* found that half the population felt that big sporting events should be stopped (52 per cent of women, 48 per cent men), while only 19 per cent felt unequivocally that they should not be (10 per cent women, 28 per cent men). Horse racing was top of the hit-list, and the spectacle of crowded car parks at race meetings on newsreel films drew much comment. One Newmarket man wrote to *The Times* in May 1941 to complain that 'thousands of gallons of petrol must have been consumed' by 'hundreds of motor omnibuses and cars converging on Newmarket from a wide area'. When Herbert Morrison admitted in the House of Commons that 'the large accumulation of cars at sports functions ... has undoubtedly been offensive to public feeling', the MPs cried 'Hear! Hear!'. A popular film of the time, *San Demetrio, London* about an oil tanker, included the captain's bitter complaint, after braving the seas and the U-boats to bring this valuable cargo to port: 'That ought to be enough to take quite a few racegoers to Newmarket.'

In general, the spectator sports provoked the most criticism, although more understanding views existed. Many argued that the war effort was not impaired and that sport played its part in taking people's minds off immediate troubles, at home and abroad. Strained and tired war-workers needed relaxation and soldiers on leave needed entertainment, and sport could provide just that.

The public were, to a degree, being manipulated. Although he was by no means a fan of Cripps, Beaverbrook recognised that this was an 'issue' that could sell his papers. A popularly accepted truth that the nation was opposed to

waste in wartime was extended to the proposal that big sports events were wasteful. Therefore, by this flawed logic, big sports ought to be banned.

Some defenders of sport pointed out at the time that more pernicious areas of waste might go unnoticed. If the government allowed petrol to be used for leisure activities or other purposes not directly related to national services without a clear directive as to what was acceptable, then it was just as reasonable to make use of them to go racing or to the dogs as to the cinema or for a day in the country. Sports events merely gathered more motorists in a single point (the car park) at one time than, say, the cinema, which was not under threat. Few films could claim to have contributed more to the war effort than, say, a football match or a boxing bout. Both sport and films were there to entertain the public.

Indeed, there was no clear evidence that watching sports had any harmful effect on war work. On Thursday 26 February 1942 there were about 3,000 present at a dog meeting at Stamford Bridge. A random sample of the crowd found none who were war workers on day shifts, although there were a few better-off people there. It became evident that the press and government campaign against sport was essentially bogus; the government had felt obliged to make some statement on the matter. The *Daily Express* ran its own sample at a dog meeting and found it basically in line with the one from *Mass Observation* quoted above. Instead it shifted its approach, claiming that much of the betting was done by 'refugees with rolls of fivers'. It could not be forgotten that sports coverage, however attenuated, helped to sell newspapers.

The whole campaign against sport was something of a failure. Churchill himself had given his powerful sanction of sporting activity by attending some big football matches. After the war, Pelham Warner, in his history of Lord's, wrote that it was 'realised by the government and the Services that cricket provided a healthy and restful antidote to war strain. .... I had the feeling that if Goebbels had been able to broadcast that the war had stopped cricket at Lord's it would have been valuable propaganda for the Germans.' Sport helped to preserve Britain's self-image and the government recognised this: Ernest Bevin asked Warner to take a team to the north after Dunkirk, in the hope that cricket would help to restore morale.

Occasional remarks continued to be made about sport's irrelevance to the major task, but the MCC President, Stanley Christopherson, urged colleagues to 'ignore these people who do not understand what we are doing'. Some even went so far as to suggest that professional sportspeople should be counted as belonging to a 'reserved occupation' and thus not liable to the call-up. After all, they did more for the nation's morale than the curates and watchmakers who could take this option. The Government spent £50,000 on a poster campaign urging cheerfulness, and many agreed that a

*Spectators were criticised in some quarters; but nobody could seriously have expected these worthies to be on the pitch.*

decent weekend's sports programme was worth a great deal more than that.

However, most sportspeople joined up without any thought of special treatment and many were made physical training instructors. So, although servicemen tended to resent early morning PT, they were often much happier about it if the instructor was a major sportsman. True, some resented the fact that instructors were non-combatant and they could often get plenty of time off to play sport – even for extra money – but this was a war in which dangers were commonly shared. There was nowhere that one could escape from it, not even in Torquay, where a remedial hospital to which Dan Maskell was attached (described by Lord Haw-Haw as a 'great military establishment in the south-west of England') received a direct hit on a night when he was off-duty.

Some people, of course, are not interested in sport anyway; many must have shared war historian Norman Longmate's pleasure at the disruption of compulsory school games. They did not care what other people got up to, so long as it did not involve them personally. The novelist

Anthony Powell, in the wartime sections of his *Dance to the Music of Time* books, was possibly of a similar persuasion. Sport is barely mentioned, but one incident is revealing. A company of soldiers refuses to play soccer among themselves:

'The boys wouldn't want that.'
'Why not?'
'Another company's what they want to beat.'

That was a good, straightforward point of view – no pretence that games were anything but an outlet for power and aggression; no stuff about their being enjoyable as such. You played a game to demonstrate that you did it better than someone else.

The dissenting voices had not come from those who cared for or understood sport. The public came to recognise this fact and continued to play and watch sports as far as their inclinations took them.

# FORTRESS BRITAIN: THE WAR AT HOME

BY the end of 1940, non-professional sport had adopted the pattern which was to continue throughout the war of mostly locally-based events against other clubs and services sides. The latter were particularly popular, because they could often contrive to bring tea with them, which helped eke out the rationing.

Although there is plainly no hard-and-fast line, a distinction can be drawn between events that were primarily designed for the forces themselves – as part of fitness training – and those events that were put on (like cricket, soccer, racing and boxing) for civilian entertainment, war charities, or to help build a rapport with the places where the forces were stationed.

The virtual absence of sports reports, in both national and local newspapers, should not be taken as proof that sport was as limited as its reporting. There were print restrictions, but one of the major limitations was that reporters could not always disclose the location of any service unit, nor the whereabouts of well-known people. Local organisers would often receive a phone call, asking if they could give 'X' unit a match a few days later. Whenever possible the locals would accept because the forces could usually provide the food for tea, the ball and petrol for the mower – items often in short supply. Teams were not selected, but compiled from a regular nucleus supported by available schoolboys, members on leave and isolated servicemen.

These games could prove to be very special, as one report from Dorset illustrates:

One memorable occasion was when T. F. Smailes, the Yorkshire fast bowler, who was stationed with a small isolated unit nearby, played for us, while our wicketkeeper was a 13-year-old evacuee schoolboy. This young lad lapped up the advice from the county man, keeping brilliantly, taking four smart catches, and inspiring the whole side (even the veterans) to field particularly keenly. The visiting side rose to the challenge and brought the game to an exciting conclusion from which we all went away with joy in our hearts.

Another village, Yately in Hampshire (which also supplied the tea provisions and petrol for the mower), hoped 'that as a village team we were able to give pleasure to members of the Forces before they went on active service'.

The little perks were very important, and certainly helped cement relations between the services and the communities. Mrs Ann Richmond recalls how, when she was a very little girl, Naval teams from Harwich and Parkstone used to play soccer in a nearby field where there were no facilities and so the sailors had to change their kit

ABOVE *After bomb-damage at Old Trafford, Manchester United moved to Maine Road for home games.*

RIGHT *Lillywhite's store provided sports equipment for the troops – and a slightly superior cut in uniforms.*

behind the bushes. Her job was to guard their uniforms when they were playing. She would try on their hats and shoes, which gave her a sense that her job was quite important. This was happily confirmed when, at the end of the game, she was rewarded with a bar of chocolate, which in wartime was priceless.

Shortages of equipment and suitable clothing were a problem. N. C. Garrett of Lillywhite's was required (until the NAAFI took over the role in 1942) to supply the services as well as the public with all they wanted, putting their slogan, 'Lillywhite's have probably got it', very much to the test. Problems could be solved in any number of ways: many a soccer team was kitted out with

shorts made from blackout curtains; little Welsh ladies knitted stockings for the England team; ladies' hockey teams bought up surplus WRNS blouses on the market and dyed them in club colours. One team in Ipswich had to fill in numerous forms simply to acquire some white paint for the hockey balls. The surplus was sold to someone who owned a boat for which he could find no paint.

Queen's club had prudently stocked up with tennis balls at the outbreak of war, although eventually they had to be rationed, but it was not until the war had ended that they realised they had not paid for them. A young male tennis player had the embarrassment of queueing with a group of

UNIFORMS
BY
LILLYWHITES
Piccadilly Circus, S.W.1

**W.R.N.S. A.T.S. W.A.A.F.
M.T.C. F.A.N.Y. W.V.S.**

Though uniforms may not differ by a jot or button from regulation pattern, yet perfect cut and expert fitting give a smartness that is unmistakable, easily recognized. Our tailors, in the Lillywhites tradition, give this distinction to our uniforms, which are ready to wear or made to measure.

The A.T.S. and W.A.A.F. uniforms photographed are stocked in bust sizes 34, 36, 38, and both cost **7½ gns.**

*Waste not, want not ... as the NAAFI reminded servicemen and women, all sports equipment was precious.*

*A slightly peevish note creeps into this advertisement. Still, the manufacturer gets his logo printed and remains patriotic.*

mothers to buy a single nappy which he tore into strips to bind the handle of his racket. Rubber, for football bladders, cycle wheel inner- and outer-tubes and golf balls, became increasingly scarce after the fall of Singapore.

One soldier, having asked for a round of golf at Sandwich, was issued with a set of clubs and a pair of wellingtons. When he asked about the unusual footwear, he was told that all the balls were in the water hazard on the first. Two men who had dragged a pond on a golf course in Dundee in 1943 were fined after retrieving 473 balls for resale. Their punishment was due not so much to stealing as indecency: one was naked and the other in his underpants. Some took this resourcefulness too far: a young North Devon golfer, who had been at RNC Dartmouth and thought he understood these things, went to retrieve his ball from out of bounds only to discover, tragically, that the area was a minefield.

Golf probably had to struggle as much as any sport to survive. The wide open spaces were

*Though there were many shortages of equipment, traditional batmaking skills were still in demand. Rubber might be scarce, but English willow was not.*

*No, these are not PoWs, but Canadian soldiers taking up cricket, forced, for lack of clothing coupons, to wear pyjamas.*

*"Is that F P A O Q? D Z T C S calling: an urgent message from M L 25 D to A C P N 2—Please instruct B I O inform H Q M F P A forthwith if O C B T C can play golf this afternoon with D A D W R S."*

attractive not only to artillerymen, who fancied using the greens as targets for practice, but also to people who wanted to plough up the courses altogether. *Golf Monthly*, however, did not regard this as a serious threat 'for any club that faces the situation in a sane and sensible manner', but the magazine did not specify how this was to be done. Instead, it recommended that golfers should go out into the fresh air and remove the strains and stresses of war before taking 'full advantage of the light chatter and happiness at the nineteenth hole'.

Golfers, like many other sportspeople, have a specialised sense of humour. Following enemy action during the Battle of Britain, when a number of players were apparently attacked by enemy bombers (not an unique experience, although it was more often by fighters), Major G. L. Edsell, secretary of St Mellons Golf and Country Club, issued some local war rules, which were generally adopted, although Richmond Golf Club also came up with something similar:

1. Players are asked to collect bomb and shell splinters from the fairways to save these causing damage to the mowers.
2. In competitions, during gunfire, or when bombs are falling, players may take cover without penalty for ceasing play.

3. The positions of known delayed-action bombs are marked by red and white flags placed at reasonably, but not guaranteed safe distances from the bombs.
4. Shell and/or bomb splinters on the greens may be removed without penalty. On the fairways, or in bunkers within a club's length of a ball, they may be moved without penalty.
5. A player whose stroke is affected by the simultaneous explosion of a bomb or shell, or by machine-gun fire, may play another ball from the same place.

Apparently, news of these 'rules' came to the ears of Dr Goebbels, who was not renowned for his sense of humour. 'By the means of these ridiculous reforms, the English snobs try to impress the people with a kind of pretended heroism. They can do that without danger, because as everyone knows, the German Air Force devotes itself only to the destruction of military targets and objectives of importance to the war effort.' Perhaps he was rattled by the phlegmatic attitude of the British.

Restrictions were, of course, considerable, although not enough for those who disliked sport. At Queen's Club the grass courts under O'Leary, the head groundsman, remained in good condition, much to his credit. He had been called up, but the club had sufficient influence that he was exempted. Somehow cricket survived as, despite all the difficulties, a trickle of balls, bats and stumps continued to be made, and even in schools, where the demand for equipment was great, matches were rarely cancelled due to lack of equipment. Although a few rugger pitches were ploughed up, the cricket pitches remained sacrosanct in most places. But the *Luftwaffe* had less respect and inevitably some grounds were hit.

Given the loss of so many sportsmen to the services, it is not surprising that many clubs merged for the duration: Blackheath Harriers and South London Harriers athletic clubs became The

Combined Clubs (TCC), while Luton Town hockey club joined forces with the Old Dunstablians and Kent's, pooling their playing resources to become a team called the Remnants. They were able to field an excellent side and never once had to cancel a match. They were also honoured by a visit to their ground at Wardown by a Hockey Association XI, a big day for local hockey enthusiasts.

In the spirit of the times, membership rules were often bent. At Queen's Club, for example, only officers were supposed to be admitted as members. Group Captain Walter Martin, a former Canadian tennis champion and later Judge Advocate to the Forces persuaded the club to make Don McDermott, the reigning Champion, and Corporal Bruce Harrison, another top player, members. Harrison recalls that the club was pretty dilapidated. He has especially fond memories of one H. P. Buckingham, who would book a grass court for him every Saturday and Sunday. But when Hitler bombed the covered courts and, worse, the management started watering the whisky, he retired in disgust from a world that was obviously falling apart.

Arguably, the energy needed for committee infighting was simply not there. The financial director of Queen's pointed out that 'during the week we were all working, some of us had two jobs, and mostly we came to the club at weekends to play tennis, bridge, and have a drink'.

The unprecedented wartime conditions caused something of a breakthrough in 1940 at Bromley Bowls Club. Few of the members there were young enough for the services, but they had other duties such as fire-watching. A motion to allow play on Sundays was narrowly accepted (37–32) under certain conditions: there was to be no play before 2pm; no paid labour could be employed and the bar would remain closed. As some form of penance for this frivolity, the old school bell hanging in front of the club was given to the Government as part of the nation-wide collection

of metal for munitions. Nevertheless, it is remarkable that even this small step into the modern world had taken 50 years and a war to accomplish.

As well as the loss of players to the services transport restrictions caused the break-up of many traditional leagues and fixtures. Astonishingly, some touring rugby teams were able to take advantage of disrupted fixture lists. Public School Wanderers, who also played cricket, provided one-off games for thousands of schoolboys and visiting servicemen from the colonies during the war.

Perhaps surprisingly, non-service women's sport was harder hit by the war than men's sport. Netta Rheinberg kept a West London group of cricketers playing with some regularity only by drawing together the members of four clubs, but

# In Aid of the Red Cross

THERE was quite a gathering of lawn tennis enthusiasts at Queen's Club last Saturday for a series of matches in aid of a very good cause. The meeting of Jean Nicholl and Peggy Scriven, both married ladies now, was the match of the meeting. It lasted two hours, and still we do not know which is the better player. In fact it was a strenuous afternoon for all the players, for in only in one match was a decision reached, and this two-setter Mixed Doubles went to 24 games.

ALMOST PRE-WAR: The Centre Court at Queen's Club looked very gay in the hot July sun and was filled for the meeting between Miss Jean Nicholl (Mrs. E. W. A. Bostock) and Miss Peggy Scriven (Mrs. F. H. Vivian).

STILL UNDECIDED: Jean Nicholl (left) and Peggy Scriven played for two hours without reaching a decision. Miss Nicholl won the first set at 7—5 and at 8—7 had three match points only to lose the game. Miss Scriven twice had set points at 12—11, but missed them, and at 13—12 to Miss Nicholl the match was stopped.

MEN'S DOUBLES: H. Billington (left) and Flt.-Lt. W. M. Martin, the Canadian Davis Cup player, had a strenuous men's doubles with Lt. S. Ellsworth Davenport and G. P. Hughes. This match had to be left drawn after Billington and his Canadian partner had lost the first set at 4—6, won the second at 6—3, and love 1—1 in the third.

AMERICAN VISITOR: Lt. S. Ellsworth Davenport, a ranked player in his own country, partnered G. P. Hughes (just in view behind him) in the men's doubles.

INTERMISSION: Miss Yorke (left) with Mrs. Jack Lysaght and Capt. McCorvas.

J. S. OLLIFF: Squadron Leader Olliff and Miss A. M. Yoke lost to Squadron Leader D. Maskell and Miss M. E. Lamb 4—6, 6—8.

the annual Women's Cricket Association's week at Colwall was clearly out of the question. Indeed, they had enough trouble playing at all as they had to take cover from aerial machine-gunning during a match at Finchley. At Headstone Lane, the WCA played against a British Empire Eleven and Megan Lowe bowled a West Indian first ball, something which still rankled twenty years later.

It seems that women's teams found travel an even greater problem than the men's teams and so most activities had to be locally based. They continued to play because, as for men, sport enabled them to forget the stresses and anxieties of war. This was not always the case: two school hockey teams in Sussex were machine-gunned by an enemy aircraft which came out of the sun. Barbara West, one of the players, recalls: 'Very fortunately no one was hit, but I can still see the flames spurting out of the end of the plane.' Despite all these difficulties, women's hockey somehow kept its organisation in good order. Clothing coupons were allocated to clubs so that when hockey started up again after the war it was almost as if nothing had happened, members who entered for the county trials were suitably dressed.

A crucial element in these games was that they were frequently played for the war charities, particularly the Red Cross. This was true of all levels of sport, although it is not always clear whether the sports meetings were put on to raise the money, or whether money-raising was tagged onto the sport.

In 1943 the Duke of Gloucester, who was the President of the joint Red Cross and St John fund, which had been launched in October 1939, was able to announce that sport had already raised the magnificent sum of £1,000,000. These funds did not only go to British causes, but also to help the Soviet wounded on the Eastern Front and to our Chinese allies, who had been struggling against the Japanese for seven years.

It was recognised that the appeal had 'stimulated every kind of sport, giving war-workers facilities for healthy recreation, both as spectators of "big sport" and as participators in events organised by themselves'. Fortunately the sources of the money raised were all noted down, which gives us a fascinating picture of the main fund-raising sports.

| | £ | | £ |
|---|---|---|---|
| Whist, dancing and bridge | 365,478 | Boxing | 25,183 |
| | | Cricket | 22,996 |
| Billiards and snooker | 79,919 | Rugby (both codes) | 10,580 |
| Darts and bowls | 72,186 | Athletics | 9,319 |
| | | Cycling | 6,356 |
| Soccer (including £3,125 from Unity Pool) | 70,236 | American Football | 2,090 |
| | | Swimming | 1,758 |
| Golf | 67,000 | Hockey | 480 |
| Greyhound racing | 50,561 | Lacrosse | 76 |
| | | Stool-ball | 36 |

What is most remarkable about these figures (which do not give the complete list) is the importance of intimate sports and games such as whist, snooker and darts. True, famous names like Joe Davis were involved in the fund-raising, but mostly it was ordinary members of the public gathering together small sums, the collective effect of which was enormous. The charity's sports committee arranged exhibition matches by leading darts players, who frequently took on local darts league champions. The committee produced 6,000 copies of a booklet entitled *25 Ideas for Red Cross Darts Contests* further to encourage this perhaps unexpected source of revenue. The BBC helped by broadcasting commentaries of several contests.

Clearly, then, it was the cosy atmosphere of the local pub or club that did the most for the war charities, because it was here, rather than in a large

Tennis players have been handicapped by lack of equipment, but, in spite of this, large sums have been raised, both by Club Tournaments and by Exhibition Matches organised by the Sub-Committee, working under the direction of Mr. C. R. Glanvill, Chairman of the L.T.A., and organised by Mr. Nigel Sharpe.

LAWN TENNIS SCORES £22,015

Billiards and Snooker players, both professional and amateur, have co-operated with the Sports Committee to raise an impressive sum for the Red Cross. Many famous players have given exhibitions in clubs all over the country, and thousands of clubs have organised competitions.

BILLIARDS & SNOOKER SCORE £79,919

*Though proper competition had been abandoned, top sports stars played exhibitions for many charities, especially the Red Cross.*

stadium, that the community spirit was most closely felt, and this reflected itself in the level of generosity.

One of the most interesting categories is that of American Football. £2,090 was raised by three exhibition matches, showing that the sport was already popular with the spectators even if it was difficult to arrange any matches. Another fact of note is that, although greyhound racing raised over £50,000 for the fund, horse racing is not recorded as contributing anything.

In truth, despite the outcry from the war

*HM King George VI and his Consort were strong supporters of racing, and enjoyed great success as owners.*

puritans, racing had a thin time of it during the war. The following figures show this clearly:

| Year | No. of horses | No. of races | Total prize money |
|------|---------------|--------------|-------------------|
| 1930 | 4,792 | 2,302 | £832,771 |
| 1940 | 3,357 | 958 | £184,787 |
| 1945 | 3,242 | 1,120 | £363,916 |
| 1948 | 5,748 | 2,684 | £1,306,211 |

At the height of the crisis – between 19 June and 14 September 1940 – all racing was suspended. The number of horses in training and at stud was greatly reduced and by 1942 there were few courses still available. At Newmarket, except for the substitute Classics and a few other important races, entry was confined to horses trained there. Salisbury and Windsor meetings were only open to horses trained south of the Trent (Newmarket

ABOVE *All the King's horses. George VI had an outstanding season in 1942, but though Sun Chariot (right) won the 1,000 Guineas, Big Game failed in the Derby.*

LEFT *Sun Chariot winning the 1942 1,000 Guineas. HM the King, in RAF uniform, is behind the section of rail above the winning post.*

excluded); Pontefract and Stockton were for those in the north. Epsom and Liverpool courses had both been requisitioned. There was no Cheltenham Gold Cup in 1943–4.

The dissenting voices might well have managed to bring a complete halt to racing had it not been for a remarkable summer in 1942 for King George VI. Although not a compulsive racing man like his grandfather, Edward VII, he was able to gauge public feeling with great accuracy. He saw the continuation of racing as a valuable safety valve for stress, and he also recognised the importance of maintaining the bloodstock. So, to help promote the sport, he attended several meetings including two wartime Derbys. In 1942, he had in his stable two oustanding horses, Big Game and the temperamental but brilliant filly, Sun Chariot, both leased from the National Stud. Big Game, superbly built, won the 2,000 Guineas at 11–8 on, and on the next day, evens favourite Sun Chariot took the 1,000 Guineas. The King began to hope for royal success in the Derby for the first time in 33 years – and so did many of his subjects.

Wartime restrictions on travel were not easy for the Royal Family to avoid, but it was equally unthinkable that the King should be absent from a Royal Derby victory. An agricultural tour of

YET ANOTHER CHANGING FACE OF BRITAIN

RACE MEETING

THEN

NOW

LEFT Punch's 'Fougasse' was a regular observer of the sporting scene: ostentation at the races was not admired.

ABOVE In 1940, with Epsom unavailable, Newmarket, as in WWI had become temporary home to the flat racing Classics.

Cambridgeshire was arranged, which would enable the King and Queen to watch both the Derby and the Oaks. This satisfactory solution was much appreciated by a large crowd mostly in khaki or blue, even more so when Gordon Richards urged an initially reluctant Sun Chariot to be first past the post at 4–1 on in the Oaks.

But there was to be no fourth great Classic win in a row. Gordon Richards himself had a Derby hoodoo on him, never having won at Epsom or Newmarket, and Big Game, despite having been sired by the Triple Crown winner, Bahram, failed to make the distance, finishing sixth behind Lord Derby's Watling Street. The King's face momentarily showed his disappointment, but he sent for Lady Derby and offered his congratulations and asked her to tell her absent husband how sorry he was that he had not been able to see the horse win. Ironically, later that season Sun Chariot beat

Watling Street by three lengths in the St Leger.

That Derby defeat was Big Game's only reverse; he went on to win the Champion Stakes ($1\frac{1}{4}$ miles) easily, before making his contribution to the war effort at stud. Being owned by the nation, his stud fees (250 sovereigns, plus a guinea for the groom) were an asset to the country. Nominations of mares were limited to 40; 20 nominations were reserved for mares which were National Stud property, five of them for mares which the director, Mr Burrell, thought to be of higher class than average, and the remainder were picked by ballot. In 1948, Big Game was the top stallion, with 25 of his offspring winning 42 races between them, worth £40,690.

In 1938 British thoroughbreds were exported to some 42 countries. Apart from the more obvious destinations like France, the USA and Italy, horses were sent to Burma, Hungary, Poland and

Czechoslovakia. Breaking these connections – despite the fact that the horses concerned were of variable quality – cost the bloodstock industry both money and international goodwill. However, the outbreak of war did not put an immediate end to exports. In July 1940 the Aga Khan's Bahram was shipped across the Atlantic at the considerable price of £40,000. Another Derby winner, Mahmoud, was shipped for a bargain £20,000. In 1941 Cameronian, the winner of the 1931 Derby, was sold to a French breeder, Simon Guthman, whose stud had been taken over by the Germans and who wanted the horse for a new stud he was starting in Argentina. In what was a potentially very dangerous mission, the horse was duly delivered, safely and on time, by a combination of Merchant Navy and RN enterprise.

The Newmarket Derby of 1943 was won by Dorothy Paget's Straight Deal, but the two great

*The Aga Khan's second successive Derby winner (1936), Mahmoud, was shipped for breeding across the Atlantic in 1941.*

confrontations of the year were in the 1,000 Guineas and the St Leger between Lord Derby's Herringbone and Lord Rosebery's Ribbon; the respective jockeys were Harry Wragg and Eph Smith. Many thought that Ribbon had won the St Leger by at least a neck; however, this was before the days of the photo-finish, and Ribbon was adjudged second, as was the case in two other, less controversial, Classics. Still, Gordon Richards could not find a Derby winner. It was not until his last attempt in 1953, appropriately in Coronation Year, that he finally succeeded.

Even in this relatively restricted format, horse racing was nonetheless fairly complex to organise. But horses had other uses than entertaining the public. They were vital for foxhunting, which was actively encouraged by the Ministry of Agriculture on the grounds that every hen the fox did not get was one for the pot. The Ministry decreed that foxhunting should continue so as to control the fox population and to provide entertainment and relaxation for those serving in the forces. That was an unusually neat piece of official judgement,

*Foxes caused havoc to wildlife in Kent, and with 'traditional methods' reduced, the locals resorted to shooting them. 62 brushes were sold for the Red Cross.*

although the packs of hounds were often reduced to a dozen couples at most, because of the shortage of food – even when the waste from nearby military canteens or other sources could be acquired.

The Marquis of Exeter, then Lord Burghley (the ex-Olympic runner), was duly grateful to one local farmer in East Sussex for providing liberal supplies of oats for the benefit of the hunt. It was only by this sort of generosity that the hunts were able to keep going.

A Buckinghamshire woman recalls in *How We Lived Then* that 'mounted followers were necessarily few and their horses unclipped and less fit than in normal times'. There were also some

advantages to the wartime arrangements: her pack, the Old Berkeley, 'hunted on Saturdays, which it had not done before, and the small fields and the slower pace of the hunting made it an admirable school for novices and children'. But, even for country people, these were no normal times; huntsmen had to beware artillery ranges and unexploded bombs. Wilde's unspeakable had to do the unthinkable, shoot foxes, and, there being no shortage of sporting cartridges, the more edible wildlife still had their problems.

An event analogous to hunting is cross-country running, particularly in its early form of a 'paperchase' in which a front-running trail layer acted as a 'hare' and the rest as 'hounds', which is why so many athletic clubs are known as 'harriers'. For the Blackheath Harriers, now part of The Combined Clubs with the South London Harriers, war raised its own problems: dropping paper was now considered almost a mortal sin, so a trail of lime was used as a barely adequate substitute. K. N. Wilkinson, while thus laying a trail, (an august and demanding job) was called 'Floury Fred' by a group of irreverent airmen and promptly went back to running as a follower. The local farmers at Hayes were more helpful: they allowed their land to be used and even opened gaps and laid sacking across barbed wire. In this way, fresh corners of the region were discovered and pastures new delighted in. Running through beautiful countryside or chatting about the day's activities in the quiet of the clubhouse, one could easily forget that there was a war on. Until the servicemen returned and the influx of Americans and Canadians began, the average age of the runners increased considerably. One small boy, on observing the runners panting their way along, remarked: 'Fancy making those poor old men run like that'.

Sydney Wooderson, one of the fitter members of TCC, was not averse to cycling from Aldershot for a meet and then running a mile in under 4 minutes 12 seconds. He was a small man and certainly no stylist, with a high arm action and an upright carriage, but he had a tremendous leg drive and might well have been the first man to run a four-minute mile (being the world record holder) if it had not been for the war. Instead the pace was set by the neutral Swedes; Gunter Hagg and Arne Andersson were able to enjoy a regularly high standard of competition at home. The USA maintained similar high levels too, and Wooderson, with his military duties and invitational appearances, simply could not match this. In 1944 he picked up an illness which cost him four months in hospital and several more resting before he was even able to take up light training again. Nevertheless, in 1945 he managed to record a personal best

of 4.04.2 at Gothenberg, but he had possibly pushed himself too hard. Hagg and Andersson were banned after the war for alleged 'professionalism', a decision which smacked of some vindictiveness, as they both had other jobs: Andersson was a schoolteacher and Hagg was a salesman in a men's shop.

Up-and-coming youngsters included the improving Doug Wilson of the Poly Harriers and Alan Paterson, a high jumper. Wilson, later to become a distinguished journalist and an organiser of the Sports Aid Foundation, brought his time for the mile down by twelve seconds in two years and gained an English record for the $1\frac{1}{2}$ miles at 6.46.6; although the target was rarely run and undoubtedly a soft one, it was welcome to a public starved of success, particularly as he was one of sport's pin-up boys. Just before a meeting in 1945 with Hagg and Andersson, he had recorded a personal best for the mile of 4.11.4, but immediately before the race he had spent 12 hours travelling, standing in the corridor of a train. It was hardly the ideal preparation, and he was disappointing in the end. However, his effort was a good example of how sportsmen in and immediately after the war years would put themselves out to honour commitments.

Paterson, the Scottish high jumper who used the 'western roll', jumped 5 feet 8 inches while still at school in 1944. Soon after he lifted this to 5 feet 11 inches at the Rangers FC sports and, at the same event in the next year, he jumped 6 feet 3 inches for a Scottish national record. Just how much athletics has since been changed by altered techniques (the 'Fosbery Flop'), training methods and technology (the fibre-glass pole), let alone doubtfully legal substances, is evident by a comparison with the current records. However, at the time Paterson's record was admirable.

RIGHT *Sydney Wooderson, Britain's star miler. Fully competition fit, he might well have been first to the four-minute mile, but for the war.*

In May 1942, looking forward to the end of the war, E. J. Holt, the AAA's Honorary Secretary, pointed out that athletics held the advantage over team sports in that hundreds could participate in running, walking, jumping and throwing events, whereas team sports usually involved only 22, or no more than 30. The war showed that simple arrangements were often the best.

A case in point is race walking. A. D. McSweeney set up a magazine called *Race Walking Record* (despite a regulation which said that no new journals could be set up) in 1941, beginning with this admission: 'Dear Reader, it is only the enthusiast who would vote this as a propitious moment to launch a journal on sport.' Perhaps, but there was considerable activity to note. (And, if the magazine ran out of material, it could always provide other useful services such as reporting: 'Found, one gent's raincoat at Parliament Hill Fields on Oct 25th' – quite a serious matter when clothing coupons were at stake.)

Although the sport was more popular in the south, the Bradford and County Walking Association continued to hold their Bradford Walk, the oldest annual walking contest in the world, which had been held every year since 1902. The Road Walking Association, however, had in 1940 suspended National activities and affiliation. Events were therefore organised by clubs, and by bodies such as the Metropolitan Police, Trams and Trolleybuses and London Transport Buses

Spreading the message at this time of opportunity was important to the walkers. N. C. Hale, who was the national 20 miles champion and Stock Exchange London to Brighton record holder, explained the sport to a group of NCOs training to be PTIs. He took the group to the by-ways where they could abandon the idea of marching to time with a straight-arm swing and instead adopt the race walker's criss-cross arm movement and rolling hips. Apparently the group enjoyed it. Whether their superiors would have been quite so happy to see a squad 'marching' in this manner is

another matter.

Not all agreed; Harold Abrahams, in BBC's 'Sportsman's Corner' told the nation that he did not like walking. It was probably one of his less wise tongue-in-cheek remarks: Jack Crump and the Rev. D. Christie Murray put up a spirited and dignified defence of the sport, but the general view was 'who cares a hoot what Abrahams likes'. Christie Murray, who boxed, played hockey, rugby, ran and walked was, with E. A. Staker of Highgate, one of the two most influential wartime walkers. Harold Whitlock, the 30-mile record holder, was engaged in war duties. (In fact his 4-29-31.8 record, achieved at White City in October 1935, was not approved by the IAAF until seven years later. They blamed the war for the delay.)

There could be unusual obstacles: walkers in the Belgrave Harriers Open – four times round Wimbledon Common – were surprised to find trip wires on each circuit. It was not sabotage by the home supporters, but the Home Guard, who were engaged in telephone-laying exercises. Staker, one of the nation's top walkers, managed to win despite this. In a Metropolitan Police Open two walkers actually retired from the race for breaking contact with the ground, which is illegal but far from unknown. This was, the *Record* suggested,

> a new development of wartime politeness; we may find walkers dropping out of their own accord when not complying with the definition – a kind of walkers' *hara kiri*.

Meanwhile, the good work carried on, as yet another article of clothing was found by one of the walkers on Parliament Hill – this time it was a sweater.

For cyclists the war was a wonderful time, because there was very little traffic on the roads and plenty of open countryside to roam. Cycling was a truly popular sport because most people could afford a bicycle and there was nothing that could be rationed, even if some had to save up for a year to buy one.

Thousands of young men and women would be up early and meet in clubs or with friends to cycle out into the countryside together. The mode of dress was practically universal: corduroy shorts, short-sleeved shirts, or sleeves rolled up, ankle socks and cycling shoes. At weekends the Great

*With few cars on the road, and no petrol needed, cycling enjoyed a war-time boom. Frank Patterson captured a restful mood.*

West Road would be packed with cyclists heading out to places like Runnymede or Windsor Castle, if possible in the slipstream of a lorry to make things easier. A favourite stopping point was a cafe called the Better Ole, where many would break for tea and cakes to talk to others of their own age. At Runnymede, lying in the sun, after a dip in the Thames, there might be warplanes overhead. But what they were doing had, according to one of the cyclists, 'nothing to do with the so-called reality of the time. At the same time we were aware that

SEVENHAMPTON ON A COTSWOLD TOUR.

when we reached the age of 18, we would have to join the madness whether we liked it or not'.

However, the war saw a major breakthrough in organised competitive biking. Track racing fell on relatively hard times, partly because of the difficulty of obtaining good track equipment, but even so most of the races provided reasonable competition and there was a good smattering of crowds. Attendances might have been better were it not for the absence on service of stars like Ken Marshall and Reg Harris. The latter was badly burned in an incident in North Africa, yet still, despite the war and struggles with officialdom, went on to win five world titles.

The road provided the opportunity which was to change the face of British cycling. The National Cyclists Union (NCU), in the last decade of the nineteenth century, after a prolonged period of attack from the police, press and public, banned all racing on public highways. Record attempts at various distances, for individuals, continued, but time-trials, where riders are set off at intervals, were banned after Frederick Thomas Bidlake promoted a famous 'North Road 50'. He was not deterred, but realised that the events would, from then on, have to remain secret. So the races took place in the early morning, at venues identified by coded references, with participants inconspicuously dressed in a uniform of black alpaca jackets and black tights. All bikes carried a bell and obeyed the law of the land during the race, even displaying courtesy to other highway users. In 1921 the NCU changed heart and allowed road racing, although not massed-start racing.

The NCU's conservative attitudes contrasted sharply with the innovative spirit which characterised much sport during the war years. So, Percy Stallard, frustrated by the NCU's attitude to mass starts, decided to go it alone. He advertised a race from Llangollen to Wolverhampton on Sunday, 7 June 1942. The race was expected to last about $2\frac{3}{4}$ hours and Stallard had secured the permission of every chief constable through whose county the

race would pass. The NCU responded by suspending him. However, the race went off without a hitch and was won by E. A. Price of Wolverhampton Wheelers and Stallard presented £105 to charity, including £3 prize-money generously returned by Price.

The NCU reacted furiously and suspended not only Stallard but all his assistants and the riders who took part. The result was inevitable: on 15 November 1942, various groups merged to form a new body, the British League of Racing Cyclists. Their first stage race was held in Kent over three days and Les Plume was the overall victor. Chas Messenger recalls that race, which was the beginning of a new era in British cycling:

> It took place in 'doodle-bug alley' in the southeast. Any sport brought the crowds out in those days and they cheered the riders on the circuits round Tonbridge. During a 'red alert' warning all the spectators disappeared and the villages were absolutely deserted. The field of 24 riders were hammering along when two of our planes came in sight in hot pursuit of a doodle-bug. They flew parallel with the riders before banging away at the flying bomb and shooting it down into some woods. The next time the riders came through the village, the main street was again packed with cheering crowds, for the 'all clear' had been sounded.

After the Brighton to Glasgow run of 1945, His Majesty the King graciously accepted an illuminated address, and the League could not be stopped. Then followed, in time, events like the Tour of Britain, Milk Race and City Centre cycling. The enterprise of Stallard and company was crucial.

Then, as now, the most-played game of all was darts; its special combination of skill and conviviality making it possible to bring relatively large numbers together from a local area. At St Ives, Huntingdonshire, Charlie Garner, the well-known BBC darts commentator helped bring together a competition in May 1942 which involved 44 teams of four players. The event was held at the Corn Exchange and organised by the Well Wishers Club whose object was to provide a Christmas gift for the men and women of St Ives serving in the forces. The winning dart was thrown by Mr Albert Flack, of the Ship in Warboys, a district organiser in Charlie's ambitious plan to hold a county-wide championship to be finished before the end of June 1942, when new petrol rationing restrictions came into force. The competition was held in aid of Mrs Churchill's tremendously successful Aid-to-Russia Fund.

Similar tales could be told of events all over the country as funds, large and small, were gathered for charity. Indeed, darts boards seemed to be everywhere, from Home Guard post to pubs and clubs. In the same way, exhibitions of billiards and snooker by notable professionals and amateurs for various war charities were held. The demonstrations given by some lady experts were particularly successful, not only for the standard of play, but in the way they relieved spectators of charity money.

The great Joe Davis, when serious competition ended at the outbreak of war, set up a stage act, with old stage pros like Tommy Trinder and Cyril Fletcher taking a gentle rise from the wings – conditions which were hard to adjust to after the reverential silence of the snooker halls. However it worked, and in 1941 he launched the Joe Davis Penny Fund, a straightforward appeal for coppers which would add up eventually to the £550 needed to buy an ambulance for the Red Cross or St John. He toured the country with his brother Fred, until the latter went into the army, and they reached the target within months. In all, seven vehicles were bought in this way. Other players joined in round the country, often becoming expert public speakers as well as auctioneers of items as varied as pictures of Churchill, cigars and autographed cues.

At the Greyhound in Kensington Square, during a charity night for the RAF Benevolent Fund, the jockeys Steve Donaghue and Gordon Richards played a game of snooker. Every time Richards bent down to play a shot, Steve would leap on his back and ride Gordon round the table. Raymond Glendenning of the BBC was the compere and helped Davis to sell the goods: a banana, then very scarce, was put up for sale and went for £100; a bomber pilot ripped off his wings which went for another £100. In this way £1,600 was made in that one night.

Sport had a wider role in the war effort than simply raising money for charity. It was an im-

*World snooker champion, Joe Davis won a great battle against brother Fred in 1940 – and went on to perfect a stage act.*

*Fred Davis, in his quiet way, helped to keep snooker to the fore in the war years.*

the annual opportunity to visit dispersed friends and relatives was not easily removed. As with the opposition to war puritanism regarding travel to race meetings, the feeling remained that the Government should make specific directives and not just produce waffling propaganda. A report in August 1941 described the 'holidays at home' campaign as having 'developed into a broad farce'.

It was not due to a lack of sporting events. Luton Town FC staged outdoor boxing in July 1942 as part of the programme, and the big local cricket fixture between Luton Town and Vauxhall was staged on Whit Monday and August Bank Holiday each year to attract as large a crowd as possible. Warwickshire staged a number of cricket matches in the August Bank Holiday week, including a two-day match in 1942 against a strong Civil Defence XI, in which county skipper R. E. S. Wyatt made a splendid 171 not out. The Leicestershire club, despite financial and other problems, also staged a series of matches for 'holidays at home'.

Huntingdon, like many other towns, set up a Summer Games Campaign, aimed primarily at young people, which tried to introduce new sports and games which required fairly basic facilities and equipment. It was a 'have a go' idea, based around such sports as deck-tennis, volleyball, basketball, rounders and field handball, which could be played on the village green without the smooth grass needed for cricket or tennis. There were also 'keep fit' displays from the Huntingdon Centre and classes taken by Miss Wuldrum and Mr Lumley.

Much of this type of activity was the work of the Central Council of Recreative Physical Training, which had been informed by the National Fitness Council on the outbreak of war that it should terminate the lease of its office accommodation and end the contracts of all members of its staff, and so had done remarkably well to organise anything. But a delegation of Lord Hampden, Sir Percival Sharp, Stanley Rous, J. W. Catlow and Phyllis

portant part of the Government's 'holidays at home' programme which began in 1941 and aimed to reduce pressure on the transport services and the overcrowded coastal areas. Local authorities were asked to arrange events that would encourage inhabitants to stay at home. Although the scheme continued throughout the war, it was not a complete success. There were limits, even in war-time, to the amount of restrictions that could be imposed upon the British people. Researchers found that this appeal was much resented and thus ignored by many, so they suggested that there was 'a definite need for a national campaign directed at keeping the middle class at home'.

However, the urge to escape from familiar, and often bomb-damaged, surroundings and to take

Colson went to the Board of Education and persuaded them that the Council should continue its work and develop an 18-month programme of activity. The Board itself produced a circular which began:

> The social and physical development of boys and girls between the ages of 14 and 20 who have ceased full-time education has for long been neglected in this country. . . . The Government are determined to prevent the recurrence during this war of the social problem which arose during the last. They have accordingly decided that the Board of Education shall undertake a direct responsibility for youth welfare.

The circular announced that financial assistance was being provided which would include grant-aid to the Central Council of Recreative Physical Training, 'for carrying on the Council's valuable work in maintaining and developing the supply of trained leadership in all forms of recreational activity'. Thus, although still a voluntary body, the Council was also an agency of the state. (At its AGM in January 1944, they resolved to change the title to the Central Council of Physical Recreation, a name carefully chosen to imply their autonomy.)

Its first major campaign, 'Fitness for Service', organised for young men, was an immediate success and by the end of July 1940 some 35,000 had taken part in PT, boxing, other games and some pre-military training. Another new idea was a Summer School at Lowther College in North Wales. The school ran for six years and produced a number of 'junior leaders' (many of them women), trained to encourage young people into action. Other courses were soon organised.

Of course, the main aim of the programme was to improve the war effort. The Council reported that 'the main preoccupation is to ensure maximum output. As the war progresses, production will be increasingly governed by the stamina of the workers. A director of a factory which allows its women employees to take part in keep-fit classes during working hours writes that the classes, though short, have already proved valuable to women sitting all day at benches.'

Early in August 1940, the President of the Board of Education announced in the House of Commons that a small Directorate of Physical Education was being formed to 'work in close association with the Youth Branch of the Board and in co-operation with the War Office'. It was hoped that the Directorate would help to improve the poor levels of fitness among school-leavers; Phyllis Colson was specially recruited to the DPE because the President, Herwald Ramsbotham, believed that 'if this Directorate is to do its work at all efficiently, we should have the services of an experienced and competent Woman Officer to look after the girls' and women's side'. One of the more remarkable recommendations of the Directorate was 'to secure the release from the Army of men suitably qualified and willing to return to civilian life to help with physical recreation for young people'.

The Council kept a general overview of attempts to set up various national proficiency award schemes, but these did not come to full fruition – outside the realms of one particular sport, swimming – until the Duke of Edinburgh's Award began in 1956. A panel was set up under Stanley Rous to advise the BBC on broadcasting early morning exercises. Perhaps 1,500,000 people responded to the call from Coleman Smith and May Brown to get 'Up in the Morning Early'. Ann Driver's 'Music and Movement' was aimed at encouraging the athletic spirit in younger listeners.

One of the unlikely upshots of the war, on the face of it, was the matching of a Rugby League team against a Union team. Yet this happened twice, under Union rules, at Headingley, Leeds on 23 January 1943 and at Odsal, Bradford a year later. The League side won both matches, 18–11 and 15–10, with the proceeds going to charity.

Rugby League, like most other sports, struggled to continue during the war because most players were recruited to the services and very few managed to become PTIs, which would have increased their availability. About half of the League's clubs, mostly in Yorkshire, continued to operate with the aid of guest players in an emergency competition. There was no Challenge Cup in 1940, but a strong Leeds team beat Halifax in the finals of 1941 and 1942. In the Leeds team were Eric Batten, who would play in four Wembley finals for Bradford Northern and Featherstone, Johnnie Lawrenson of Wigan and the great Salford pair Alan Edwards and Gus Risman. Leeds were beaten in a two-leg final in 1943 by a Dewsbury team which included guests from a good pre-war Salford side: Barney

Hudson, Alan Edwards and George Curran. It was managed by Eddie Waring, the inimitable BBC commentator. In two more double-legged finals, Bradford Northern beat Wigan in 1944 and were beaten by Huddersfield the next year. There were no Test matches during the war years, but an England side played Wales six times, winning three, drawing two and losing one.

There were a number of Union 'internationals',

RIGHT Punch's *view, 1945.*

BELOW *If raising 11 soccer players was hard, 15 rugby players was even more difficult. For the Universities there was less of a problem, undergraduates in residence were easily available for a 1941 Varsity match.*

but these were really services' matches, sometimes held at expected places like Swansea, Leicester and Murrayfield, but occasionally at strange venues such as Wembley and Inverleith. The games aroused great interest among the general public who, as ever, welcomed any change from the dreary days of war. Otherwise, games continued to be arranged through a mixture of service, club and individual initiative.

Wartime restrictions hit most of the larger amateur sports. There were no major swimming competitions, so the sport was reduced to galas and an educational role. However, one must not ignore Miss N. Riach's remarkable summer in 1944 when she set five British records over five distances between 100 and 440 yards.

The Amateur Rowing Association reported a 'general picture of informal regattas wherever there were oarsmen or oarswomen. Many of these were in aid of the Red Cross or some other charity'. Boat club facilities were sometimes required for war use – one club was forced out of its boathouse at Barnes so that it could be used as a mortuary; Eton College offered to share its facilities at Henley with Shrewsbury School. There were four Oxford v Cambridge boat races. The standard was inevitably low and no Blues were awarded. Ice, snow and a 'flu epidemic hampered preparations for the first, held at Henley, which Cambridge won with some ease. Because of disagreements about qualifications in 1941 and Oxford's failure to raise a challenge in 1942, two years were missed. In 1943 a race was held at Sandford, near Oxford, apparently attracting between 7,000 and 10,000 spectators. Cambridge slipped at the start and never recovered the length they lost. The next race, over the Adelaide course at Ely, was watched by 5,000 who saw an exciting struggle in which Oxford pulled away to win by three-quarters of a length. The final wartime race was held at Henley over the full regatta course and Cambridge won by two lengths, to leave the war record square at two each.

Motor-cycle speedway, apart for some racing at Rye House, was concentrated at Belle Vue, Manchester from the end of the 1940 season. Riders struggled there from all over the country for the Saturday meetings. Some brought their bikes onto already overcrowded trains or hitched lifts on lorries, while others left them at Belle Vue. The local contingent was led by Frank Varey, Bill Kitchen and Oliver Hart. From the Midlands came the Parker brothers, Alec Statham, Bill Pitcher and Les Wotton. Regulars included Eric Chitty, Tommy Price, Ron Johnson and newcomer Ron Clarke.

There were races between individuals, pairs and a few team matches. In 1943 and 1944, a miniature league was formed in which Belle Vue, assisted by some guest riders, took on an Opposition selection. The premier event of the year, however, was the British Individual Championship, run on World Cup lines, with preliminary rounds and a final. Eric Chitty won three times in succession (1940–2); next year he did not qualify for the final, which was won by Clarke, who was succeeded by Varey (1944) and Kitchen (1945). All the riders, if not in the services, were engaged in some form of war work and had to show great determination to carry on with their sport. Despite this, the organisers felt obliged to post notices that speedway fuel could not be better used for the war effort in more conventional bikes, to pre-empt any criticism.

One professional sport to take some advantage of the war was wrestling. It had a very bad pre-war image and had been banned from London County Council premises. By skirting the centre, and putting on shows for charity at places like Beckenham baths, promoters like Les Martin and Johnny Dale began to improve the public's perception of the sport. The wrestlers were themselves often engaged in the tiring and unpleasant ARP duties of heavy lifting after bombing raids, which did their reputations no harm at all.

Boxing, both amateur and professional, con-

*Jack 'Kid' Berg, world junior welterweight
champion in 1930, fought as a pro for 21 years, and
was a popular performer in the wartime ring.*

*British lightweight champion Eric Boon, wearing the
Lonsdale Belt, which became the focus of acrimony
between promoters and the Board of Control.*

tinued to flourish except at the highest levels.
Promoters were nervous from the start about
staging championship fights, as they reckoned
they would be lucky to break even after paying tax,
levy, expenses and purses. Indoor fights were
usually held in the afternoon, thus drawing the
wrath of the war-puritans who thought people
should be working. Those held outdoors risked
cancellation because of weather conditions. Smaller London venues such as the Cambridge Theatre
and the Alexandra Theatre on Hackney Road were
used, but top fighters such as Kid Berg, Eric Boon,
Alf Phillips and Dave Crowley appeared there and
boxed for real rather than taking the easy option of

staging exhibition bouts. However, exhibitions
were widely popular, even though the crowds
often commented scathingly on the contrast between the all-action amateurs and the more circumspect professionals.

Amateur boxing also continued, although the
ABC Championships were occasionally staged at
Belle Vue, and the number of events was reduced.
Reg Gutteridge fought in an ARP competition in
Walthamstow – no canvas, directly on grass. He
recalls his fight in the flyweight final during an air-
raid on the docks:

We could actually see the German bombers

coming up the Thames and hear the gunfire going and the barrage balloons being lifted. The opponent and I kept looking at one another and looking at the sky at the same time. We didn't actually get the decision in the ring – we all rushed back under the stands, and they gave it in the dressing rooms. I won, but possibly because my dad and uncle were in the opposing corners, so I think they had an influence on the judges.

The great fight of the war was held on 20 June 1942 in the open air at White Hart Lane, Tottenham, between the champion, Pilot Officer Len Harvey, and Flight Sergeant Freddie Mills for the British and Empire light heavyweight titles. Such matches are made in heaven: the public was starved of top boxing and there could hardly have been a greater difference between the two competitors. Harvey was 34, skilful, experienced and a gentleman, while Mills was 12 years his junior, an ex-milkman from Bournemouth and an all-action fighter not noted for subtlety. There was, however, a problem: under the existing regulations officers could not fight against other ranks. Under pressure from Mills' insistent new manager, Ted Broadribb, and public opinion, the rules were rewritten. It was another small sign of the flexi-

*Freddie Mills on the attack against Len Harvey. For an NCO to fight an officer was previously unheard of. The rules were changed.*

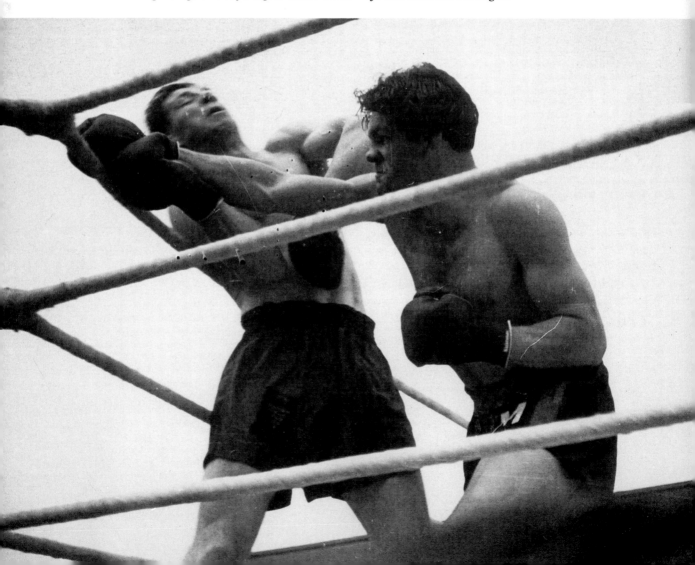

bility induced by wartime conditions.

Harvey was clear favourite; the former fly-weight champion of the world, Jimmy Wilde, explained why he thought he would win: 'He is a past-master in ringcraft, possesses an almost impregnable defence and is seen at his best when opposing less clever opponents.' Other writers, however, noted that Harvey had not fought for three years. Frank Butler said in the *Daily Express* that the key lay in Harvey's legs ('the most talked about in Britain' – except, perhaps, for those pertaining to Mesdames Dietrich and Grable). However, all agreed that it would be a long, tough fight.

Mills was encouraged by his manager to train in the open at the Airman Hotel, Feltham. Spectators could come to watch him for a few pence donated to charity. This not only acclimatised Mills to likely conditions, but helped to establish him as a popular fighter. Meanwhile Harvey, after his

*Len Harvey was dumped out of the ring by Freddie Mills in the title fight for the Lightweight Championship in the second round.*

training, sat listening to Gigli records and went into the ring as 3–1 on favourite.

There were 30,000 spectators at Tottenham that night. The first round was evenly balanced, but Harvey surprised the fans at the start of the second by carrying the fight to his young opponent. Suddenly, as Harvey was retreating, Mills hit him with a tremendous left hook to the jaw. Harvey was sent down for a count of eight. Mills saw his chance and stormed into the attack, finally depositing the champion outside the ring. The fight had lasted just under four minutes.

There was pandemonium: Len Harvey's distressed wife had to fight her way to get to her husband's side after Mills' hand had been raised. Immediately after the fight was over a red rose was

*Flight Sergeant Freddie Mills makes a point. Sport cut across social barriers, and sportsmen could sometimes 'get away with murder'.*

thrown into the ring and presented to the winner. In Mills' room naturally, there was more excitement, with his closest family struggling to get in and join the celebrations.

The problem for Mills was that there was nobody at his weight that could provide decent opposition. He was a national personality but needed much more than exhibitions to keep him ring-trim and in the public eye. So Broadribb decided that Mills would aim for the British heavyweight title, but a match with the champion Jack London proved hard to arrange. There was slightly wild talk about a contest with Joe Louis, then in Britain touring with a US forces-sponsored group, but the Americans decided that such a match would be against their regulations. This was probably just as well for, although Louis was now possibly past his very best, he successfully defended his world title four more times, before retiring undefeated in 1948. When Mills did eventually climb into the ring with Louis, it was only to referee one of the 'Brown Bomber's' exhibitions. At another US camp, the referee told young Mills that he had a fair chance of winning the world cruiserweight championship, but recommended that he stayed at light heavyweight. He was delighted at this advice from Jack Dempsey, the former world heavyweight champion; but did not heed it.

At last the fight against Jack London for the heavyweight title was arranged. London was three stones heavier, but had been beaten in a previous bout by Mills, who was now favourite. The match took place on 15 September 1944 at Belle Vue but, in what was regarded as one of the finest heavyweight fights ever seen, Mills (having made the early pace) finally ran out of steam and lost on points. After the war Mills took the world light heavyweight title from the American Gus Lesnavitch in London in 1948. He did not keep it for long and retired to a world of showbiz and fame in the clubs of Soho in 1950. He died on 24 July 1965 in a shooting incident which has never been satisfactorily proven as suicide or murder.

1941–2 was probably the toughest time of the war in Britain. The blitz was at its height and most commodities were scarce; news from the Mediterranean was often depressing, while that from the Far East was disastrous; there was direction of labour and conscription for women. The people rallied round with an unique determination. They accepted 'utility' standardisation and the idea that all should be channelled towards the war effort. Sports goods were inevitably put under scrutiny, but it was not suggested that their manufacture should be ended, only that their use and distribution should be monitored. In the case of cricket,

*Freddie Mills v Jack London, fighting for the British heavyweight title in 1944. Mills, though much the lighter was favourite, but London ground him down in an enthralling points win.*

the county clubs were requested to work out their local clubs' priorities. Some cricket historians regard this as a missed opportunity to set the game up at a truly national level, but this was simply not possible at the time.

The MCC decided to continue with the same approach as had been adopted for the 1940 season. *Wisden*, at least, seems to have regarded the Tom Brown Centenary Match as the chief game of the season. An MCC team took on Rugby School, as it had done 100 years earlier when Thomas Hughes, Brown's creator, had captained the school in the first ever game against MCC which ended excitingly with the boys needing 14 to win with one wicket in hand. The 1941 MCC side was very strong and included Bob Wyatt, Errol Holmes,

'Gubby' Allen and the formidable hitter, Jim Smith. The school's bowlers acquitted themselves well, keeping MCC down to 149–9; but Wyatt (4–14) and Smith (6–8) were too much for the boys, who were scuttled out for 31. L. G. H. Hingsley missed the group photograph, because he had been bombing German factories until 5 am, and was bowled for a duck.

The Army and the RAF, the two strongest services' sides, staged five games at Lord's, Sheffield, Nottingham, Harrogate and Liverpool. The Army won two games, the RAF three. It was noted that, to take advantage of dewy conditions available with 11 am starts during double British Summer Time, many captains put their opponents in first. This was a lesson re-learned by modern one-day captains to the chagrin and discomfort of opening batsmen.

No such excuse could be provided for the King's College School Wimbledon, however, at Dulwich College. The home team went in first and

*Rugby School and the MCC celebrated in 1941 the centenary of their first encounter, which was immortalised in* Tom Brown's Schooldays. *Though the boys were trounced by a strong MCC team, the cricketing idyll continued, but most boys were soon in more serious action.*

scored a comfortable 171–6 with Trevor Bailey making an undefeated 84. Kiddle tore into KCS taking eight wickets for just three runs, including a hat trick in what was regarded as a public school record. The visitors were all out for 10.

London Counties enjoyed another successful season, losing only three of their 38 matches and raising £1,400 for charity. Two useful recruits to the Counties side were Denis and Leslie Compton, although Denis could only play occasionally. Such was Leslie's form that Robertson-Glasgow tipped him as a possible England batsman. However, despite being a solid wicketkeeper, he performed mostly in the middle order after the war, following Middlesex's almost preposterously successful first four of Robertson, Brown, Edrich and his brother, so he rarely had the chance to build a big innings. On the other hand, despite a career spent slightly in Denis's shadow, he did win a full England soccer cap, late in his career, a feat his brother

never achieved.

Another recruit was CSM A. R. Gover who joined Counties in 1941 and took 83 wickets at 9.50. A story of his neatly sums up the vagaries of wartime sport. One day Alf was playing for his unit on a public field somewhere on the south coast and there was another match taking place alongside. Alf was, perhaps unusually for him, making some runs and thoroughly enjoying himself. Suddenly, as a ball was bowled, a player from the other game hurtled across the wicket. Gover stood back and was duly bowled and given 'out'. Before leaving the crease, Gover made his displeasure known and was severely reprimanded by his captain for disputing the decision. The day after, Alf was playing at Lord's.

The Empire XI played 40 games, winning 19 and losing ten. R. E. S. Wyatt, sometimes cautious, sometimes reckless, topped the averages with 82.40, in only six games. He scored a dazzling 149 against Cambridge University as the XI failed by only seven runs with two wickets still in hand to score the 241 required in two and a half hours. Much of the consistent batting came from Harry Crabtree of Essex, his fellow-countyman A. V. Avery and A. C. L. Bennett of Surrey. Although he played for the Rest of England team against the RAF at Lord's, W. M. F. Bebbington's health and batting deteriorated so Bennett dealt with the club's affairs during the last month of the season. Bertie Clarke was the top bowler, taking 98 wickets during the season. At Imber Court he took 15–58 in a match against the Metropolitan Police, including all ten second innings wickets and a hat trick.

The 1942 *Wisden* announced – prematurely – that 'a full fixture list is being arranged for 1942,

*Trevor Bailey (centre, seated), captain of a strong Dulwich College XI, was a rising wartime star. A. W. H. Mallett and O. J. Wait also played first class cricket post-war.*

and the British Empire XI officials trust that their work will be as well supported as in the past'. Donnelly, the previous spring, had been working on ambitious projects for a nationwide tour at the end of the war, and even began to plan a tour of India under Norman Yardley, to take place if the MCC weren't prepared to organise one. However, Donnelly was 'called to the colours' in mid-season of 1941, and his ally, Bebbington, was sick. During the winter of 1941–2 the constitution was restructured; the organisation was entrusted to less mercurial fellows such as Sir Pelham Warner MBE, who became the president; Stanley Rous (who took over from Bebbington) was the new honorary secretary, Ray Smith of Essex became captain and A. C. L. Bennett completed the committee. The 1943 *Wisden*, in a piece by founder-member Reg Hayter, hints at a degree of discontent under the new arrangements. It agreed that 'the new control off the field functioned smoothly,' but regretted that 'two of the club's founders took no part in any of the activities'.

*Two touring teams in the South of England brought first-class players to outlying clubs and hugely benefited war charities. London Counties were professionals, while the British Empire XI were amateurs. The match between them was a highlight.*

Hayter also deplored the fact that the highlight of the previous seasons, the fixtures with London Counties, had been discontinued.

But it was not simply a story of club in-fighting in 1942. There were some bright spots. Trevor Bailey joined the Empire XI taking 15 wickets and scoring runs at an average of 45; and although he was young and of slight physique and tended to tire quickly, it was believed that if he was well coached he could develop into 'a more than useful county cricketer'. Clarke excelled himself with 129 wickets at 10.17, while the bulk of the scoring was done by Avery, Crabtree and, until he joined the Army, Bennett.

The appointment of Stanley Rous as honorary secretary to the Empire XI did not mark the end of Bebbington's involvement in cricket. He swiftly resurfaced – for the opposition. In the winter of 1942–3, the founder of London Counties, C. J. E. Jones, resigned his position as honorary secretary

owing to circumstances 'beyond his control'. Captain Foulkes, the president, led a reorganisation and Bebbington was appointed honorary secretary. Foulkes arranged with Stanley Rous (who was principal officer of the Red Cross Sports Committee), that the proceeds of all matches the next summer should go to the Red Cross and St John fund instead of supporting local charities as had previously been the case. Rous and the Red Cross had thus annexed the funding of both the major touring teams.

In 1942 the Counties lost only to Reading, thanks to a wet wicket that had improved for the Reading innings. Denis Compton headed the averages with 86.80, but played only six matches; brother Leslie scored 950 runs. His highest score was 99, when he had the bad luck to be bowled by the ninth ball of an eight-ball over, due to an umpiring error. Left-arm spinner Jack Young headed the bowling averages. Against Epsom, he achieved the hat trick twice in the course of 24 deliveries.

The great match of 1942 was between a combined Middlesex and Essex side against Kent and Surrey at Lord's. It was part of the 'holidays at home' campaign and was held over the August Bank Holiday weekend. There was a crowd of 22,000 on the Saturday. The game opened prosaically enough, but Dulwich captain Trevor Bailey, brought on with the score at 33, provided a sensation. His second ball bowled Leo Bennett, his seventh had Bridger leg-before and the eighth took out the middle stump of L. H. Todd of Kent. The game also ended sensationally: Middlesex and Essex were faced with a target of scoring 190 in just 100 minutes. They had a stolid start, but then Compton and Edrich came together and, according to *Wisden*, 'brought off every possible run, their judgement and speed between the wickets supplementing audacious strokeplay'. (This may surprise those who hold the view that a call from Denis Compton was merely an entry into negotiations; he even managed to run out his brother Leslie in the latter's benefit match.) The match ended with Compton requiring four off the last ball, but he was stumped by Godfrey Evans off the bowling of Alec Bedser. Evans was, as always, standing up to the wicket to the great fast-medium bowler.

Off the cricket field, Len Hutton injured his left arm when a mat slipped from under him on the last day of a PT course. This injury, according to his biographer Gerald Howat, prevented him from joining a commando raid on Dieppe in 1942. He had fractured the forearm and dislocated the ulna at the base of his wrist and the injury turned out to be more complicated than first thought. Although he returned to cricket in the summer of 1941, it was with great discomfort, and he was forced to abandon the game for 20 months. Surgeons grafted bone from his right leg to the forearm but this did not solve the problem and at the end of the year he had another graft from the left leg,

which was successful. However, he now had one arm almost two inches shorter than the other. For the moment, he returned to league cricket.

A sad incident at Lord's in the summer of 1942 served as a reminder that it was not only war that was a cause of human mortality. On 23 July, Andrew Ducat, aged 56, collapsed and died at the wicket while playing for the Surrey Home Guard against the Sussex Home Guard. He had been a cup-winning skipper of Aston Villa and a reliable Surrey batsman with one test to his credit when he

*Andrew Ducat, who died at the wicket at Lord's.*

faced the pace of E. A. McDonald. He was out when a ball took off the shoulder of his bat and lobbed up to Gregory in the slips. The splinter fell onto his stumps and so he was out both caught and hit wicket. The coach at Eton, he was regarded as a 'well set up, vigorous, healthy looking and careful-living man.' He did have, however, an undetected heart weakness; perhaps he should neither have been in 'Dad's Army' nor playing active sport. On the other hand, could he have asked for a better way to go?

The pattern of cricket in 1943 and 1944 was similar to that earlier in the war, with a mixed programme at Lord's; there was a smattering of county games, with Nottinghamshire prominent, spurring the others into action. The Empire XI, London Counties and star-studded midland and northern leagues continued to provide high level activity. Services matches were also popular: the RAF beat both the Army and the Civil Defence. The first match was watched by 22,000 and the second by 15,000. For the Civil Defence against the Army, the big-hitting Harold Gimblett of Somerset scored 124 in a blistering attack, which brought him 100 in 86 minutes, including three sixes and 15 fours. One hook for six sent the ball well over 100 yards, high into the Mound Stand at Lord's. He came to the match very much out of practice. He worked with the Fire Service, and although a witty raconteur among his colleagues, he was deeply upset by the death and destruction that he saw, and this must surely have influenced his eventual suicide.

Another huge crowd of 21,000, including Lord and Lady Baldwin, watched a draw between the Army and the RAF in July 1943, which was distinguished by fifties from C. S. Dempster, Maurice Leyland and 83 from Denis Compton, who was making only his first appearance of the season since Army duties and operations on both legs for varicose veins had kept him out of action. On 14 August the Army pulverised the Navy, winning by 176 runs thanks largely to Dempster's

undefeated 111. The Navy, despite fielding a side which included two new recruits, Bailey and Mallett, were palpably outgunned. Fourteen thousand watched the match and over £311 was raised for the King George's Fund for Sailors and the Army Funds. But the Army did not have it all their own way: the National Police scored 196, helped by a number of dropped catches. Jim Parks took 4–16 as the Army, including Robertson (top scorer with 38), Dempster, Charles Palmer, Hugh Bartlett, M. S. Nichols, Billy Griffith, Brian Sellers, Ian Peebles and Reg Perks collapsed to 93 all out.

There were some new formations at this time. On 29 May 1943 a strong England XI beat a West Indies team at Lord's, featuring Clarke and Constantine, but none of them in the best of practice. Alec Bedser took 6–27, including a tail-end hat-trick, despite a spate of no-balls. On a glorious day, there was a crowd of 20,000, and £321 went to the Colonial Comforts Fund. West Indies teams also played two matches in Lancashire. The County itself did not get involved, but several quality games were arranged to benefit charity and provide entertainment for 'stay-at-home holidaymakers'.

The RAAF made a fairly undistinguished first appearance at Lord's, being bowled out for 100, losing by 101 runs. Keith Miller with graceful drives and crisp cuts made 45 of them but, inevitably, C. B. Clarke and Alec Bedser got amongst the wickets with 3–22 and 3–30 respectively.

The great match of the season of 1943 was over two days, between England and the Dominions at Lord's on August 2–3. Almost 24,000 spectators were present on the Monday, and more than 14,000 watched the next day. England opened with 324 for nine declared, with a dashing 58 from Denis Compton and a splendid innings of 133 from Leslie Ames, backed by 30 not out from Trevor Bailey, who showed 'discreet defence' in a stand of 112. 'Discreet defence' would have been a very mild Colonial description of some of 'blocker Bailey's' later back-to-the-wall efforts. The Dominions then collapsed for 115 to an unlikely eight over spell from Denis Compton which brought him 6–15 with left-arm spinners. Next morning, it was England's turn to struggle, but a typically dashing 69 not out from Walter Robins led to a declaration which left the Dominions looking for 360 in about four hours. They got within eight runs of it; the New Zealander, Dempster, played a beautiful 113, and Constantine was caught for 21 by Leslie Compton actually over the boundary fence (but his feet were grounded inside), which disappointed some fans. Sismey, the Australian wicketkeeper, notched up seventy, and Bertie Clarke, never far from the action, hit 52 at number ten. The match ended with two splendid catches, by Alec Bedser and Bailey, off Jack Robertson's only over. The teams were presented to the Duke of Gloucester, and the proceeds went to the Red Cross.

The season drew to an end at Lord's in a bizarre match on 28 August. It was the now-traditional Middlesex/Essex v Kent/Surrey game, reduced to one day. It poured with rain in the morning, and the Compton brothers were released to play for Arsenal in the opening match of the football season at Charlton. Avery of Essex was unable to play, having injured himself tripping over his bag when leaving home for Lord's, and on the opposition side Arthur Fagg of Kent spent the whole day looking for *his* bag, which had been mislaid on the railway. New equipment, of course, did not come easily. However, play was possible after an early lunch, and the weakened 'home team' were scuttled for 75, a total which Ames and Eric Bedser reached without difficulty.

Although cricketing fixtures for 1944 were broadly similar to the previous year, they were set

*A Dominions XI, 1943. Growing numbers of overseas servicemen in England brought an international flavour to games at Lord's. Dr C. B. Clarke (standing, second from right) was a leading light of London Counties.*

against a very different background. June 6th saw the Allied landings in northern France: 'D-Day'. Many sportspeople were involved; amongst those concerned in the advance landings, by glider, were Billy Griffith and Hugh Bartlett. When the expeditionary force failed to turn up for some hours, Griffith was heard to ask, 'Do you think we have come on the right day?' – and then to talk cricket.

The diffusion of players, both onto the Continent and around the world, meant that some playing standards fell. London Counties, *Wisden* regretted, could no longer correctly be called a powerful and attractive combination of county cricketers. They lost three matches, although they were at least against the more formidable opposition such as the North of England. London Counties were still too much for more ordinary works teams, however. Jack Young took 9–5 (including a hat-trick) against A. E. C. Southall in the first match of the season, and 5–6 in dismissing Handley Page for 15 in the last. Several club

players had to be recruited, which lessened the team's attraction, though they raised over £1,000 for Lady Kemsley's War Relief Fund. They still tried to play attractive cricket, and skipper Joe Hulme made 1,034 runs – 471 of them in his last seven innings.

The Empire XI also began to lose matches. Two clubs beat them – Catford Wanderers and Merton, who included Gregory, Barling and Fishlock of Surrey – and also a strong Army side for whom Roley Jenkins took 6–61. The chief batsman was Crabtree, who, with 1,086 runs, became the first Empire player to score 1,000 in a season, and Clarke took his inevitable 102 wickets (along with averaging 26.69 with the bat). The team managed to travel considerably, with fixtures in South-

*Cricket in the West of England revived towards the end of the war. The West's fixture list was mostly local, but a strong team played a Lord's XI in July 1944.*

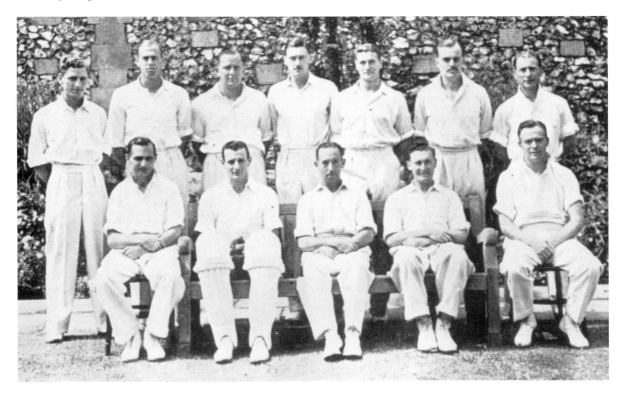

*July 29th 1944, and a VI flying bomb – 'doodlebug' – passes overhead, threatening Lord's. Batsman Robertson retaliates with a six.*

ampton, Eastbourne, Coventry and new areas such as Cardiff, where Glamorgan had been staging something of a revival.

One of the major new areas of play was the West Country, which in 1944 saw a vast increase in activity, despite setbacks and disappointments caused by bad weather and last minute changes of plans by the military. This was due largely to the West of England XI's secretary, G. O. J. Elliott, a Gloucester Club member who had been invalided out of the Army. He was also forced to take over the captaincy on a number of occasions; the players insisted and to show their appreciation of all he had done, presented him with an inscribed silver cigarette box.

Considerable travel problems were overcome (it was not unknown for trains to be so full that the players got left behind on the platform!) and although performances were sometimes modest, large crowds assembled across the country – from Reading to the South Midlands and Yeovil. In 1944, H. Storer of Derbyshire headed the averages for batting at 79.00 in six innings, and Tom Goddard took 37 wickets. An attractive game at Gloucester, between the West of England and the

Royal Air Force (captained by a returned Walter Hammond, who made 69), ended in some confusion when stumps were drawn a quarter of an hour before the scheduled time. What turned out to be the final over, from R. E. S. Wyatt, was a maiden, which left the RAF needing only three runs to win, and four wickets in hand. Nonetheless, 5,000 people raised £380.

Wyatt was also at the centre of what was probably the most celebrated cricket event of the war. 1944 was the summer of the flying bombs, the pilotless planes and rockets which turned up at all times and in all weathers and were aimed chiefly at London. The first fell on 13 June and they rapidly inflicted major casualties. By the end of July, a million and a half people had left on a more or less voluntary evacuation. Cricket at Lord's continued, although with much smaller crowds than in the previous year. On 29 July, the Army were batting against the RAF; a flying bomb approached and seemed certain to land on the Nursery Ground.

The players flung themselves to the earth, and the unpredictable bomb dropped around Regent's Park. On the resumption of the game, Jack Robertson promptly hooked Bob Wyatt for six amid tremendous cheers. Robertson explains this departure from his normal classic decorum on his annoyance both at the interruption and at the enemy.

Liverpool, Manchester United, Bath, Lovell's Athletic and Aberamon Association Football Clubs have one thing in common. They all competed in the second, post Christmas, Championship of the Football League (North) from 1943 to 1944. Bath, helped by many guests like Stanley Mortenson, actually won it with 34 points from 21 games. Aberamon, whose only previous claim to fame had been as the nurturing ground for Bryn Jones (who still played the occasional game for old times' sake) finished bottom with three points from 18. Lovell's, the team of a toffee factory (which effectively replaced the withdrawal of Newport County), were in the middle years of the war probably the strongest of the teams of this sort. They were not only included in the full League competition, but were part of a Western League which sought to keep soccer alive in the company of Bristol City, Cardiff and Swansea. The single sheet that was Lovell's programme advises: 'Make the best use of your sweet coupons and buy Lovell's Toffee Rex – still the king of toffees.' One wonders what Everton, known as the 'toffee men', must have made of that.

A chief reason behind this odd competition was the eventual revolt of the London area clubs. 1940–1 had been a difficult season. At the Annual General Meeting of the Football League in July, it had been decided that there would be two groups, Leagues North and South. There would be no professionalism, trophies or medals. The clubs objected to the last proposal; they argued that no payment would mean no well-known players, and thus no crowds. That proposal was dropped.

However, a radical structural organisational change was adopted; no points were to be awarded for wins or draws, and the leagues would be decided on goal average. Clubs would make up their own fixture lists, but first and second division clubs would have to play at least two third division teams per season. It was hoped that each club would play at least twenty matches. No attempt would be made to replay abandoned games – scores would stand as results. Eventually, with some reluctance, it was agreed to adopt a 'spotter' system which allowed matches to continue during air raid alerts, after sirens had sounded. The 'spotters' came back into service in 1944 during flying bomb alerts. Convention was also broken when the FA sanctioned Sunday football. With many men working at least six days a week, there was much pressure for this. Denis Howell, the best and most remembered Minister for Sport, recalls how he inserted an advertisement in the *Birmingham Mail*, saying that those people who wished to play on Sundays should come to a meeting at the Chamber of Commerce to set up a Birmingham 'Sunday Friendly League'. The wise local county FA representative, rather than exactly turning a blind eye, came up with an unique solution. He persuaded Billy Rogers, an ex-music hall comedian who had run a Monday League for butchers in the Birmingham markets, to set up a 'Birmingham Monday League Sunday Section', which he duly sanctioned. Such adventurous pragmatism became unnecessary, though Manchester City never got through their plan for Sunday Football League matches.

The London area clubs staged their own Cup (in which Reading beat Brentford 3–2 at Stamford Bridge before a disappointing crowd of 9,000). The full League Cup drew 60,000 to Wembley, where Preston and Arsenal drew 1–1. The 40,000 terrace tickets were sold within 24 hours, so there could be no doubt about soccer's continued pulling power. At Ewood Park, Blackburn, Preston won the replay 2–1 three weeks later, the delay

being to accommodate service matches. Next season came the big shake-up. The eleven London clubs plus Aldershot, Reading, Brighton, Watford and even Portsmouth, opted for their own competition. Crewe Alexandra also withdrew, with some reason, after having been designated to a League South that would have involved journeys to possibly Southampton and Luton. In the end, the League South was decided on the number of points, on average, that the teams would have got if they had played 18 matches – only Luton and Walsall got that far; Norwich played only eight, but nonetheless finished fourth. Leicester were the winners, with an adjusted 26.40 points from 17 games; they actually scored 25. The London League was, on the other hand, much more orderly, with 30 matches played apiece, Arsenal taking the title with 48 points.

*Empty stands at White Hart Lane for Arsenal v Charlton tell the story. Confusion about teams' make-up, including guests, and new League systems were a major factor. Slowly, the numbers grew.*

The London War Cup Final at Wembley saw Brentford beat Portsmouth 2–0 before 72,000 spectators. By then the London rebels and the League had patched up their quarrel. In 1942–3, the London Clubs played effectively the same formation as League South: Arsenal won. Watching a match now cost generally 1/3d, including Entertainments Tax, and at Christmas 1942 – the end of the first half of a double-competition league season – 35,000 watched the Wednesday v United Sheffield Derby, while on Boxing Day a total of 323,000 watched the opening cup qualifying matches. In the New Year's Honours List, Stanley

ABOVE *There was no shortage of spectators for Internationals at Wembley. For security reasons, all traces of snow had to be painted out.*

RIGHT *Snow on their boots – it had to go, even when involving Mrs Churchill. Proceeds from England v Scotland went to her Russian Aid Fund.*

Rous received the OBE.

The size of crowds continued to increase. Although the Government were adamant about continuing the Entertainments Tax, Christmas saw 320,000 spectators for the end of the first competition and 440,000 for the opening Cup and League South games on Boxing Day 1943. The North Cup was a confusing affair, with the games also counting as league matches; in the event of a draw, the 90-minute score stood as the League result, while the players went on into extra time for the concurrent Cup match. In the light of such peculiarities, Bath's winning of the season's second North Championship in 1944 seems entirely logical. Tottenham won the South title, and in the League South Cup, 85,000 at Wembley watched Charlton beat Chelsea 3–1. Aston Villa beat Blackpool 5–4 on aggregate in the North Cup, their own leg producing a 50,000 crowd.

The guest player system caused confusion and

some acerbity, but the public did not appear to mind too much. That there should be ten team changes from those announced in the programme ceased to worry; A. N. Other, A. G. (Guest) Player, 'Newman', and, for Fulham, 'S. O. Else' featured frequently. Sometimes the Press connived by attributing goals to other players when the actual scorers should have been with their units. Stanley Rous recalled his gratitude to the service officers who helped secure release for England players, and also to the soldiers and sergeants who agreed to switch duties so that these players could get away.

Not all emergency measures were successful. Brighton turned up at Norwich with half a team, scavenged some local reserves and lost 18–0. Goalkeeper Sam Bartram hitched a lift on a fire engine, but still missed the kick-off. Charlton played a local milk-deliveryman, thinking he was the expected guest. A certain amount of 'head-hunting' went on. George Murphy of Bradford City – not one of the great names – reckoned he played for eight different clubs in nine weeks; there was a mercenary element. Even if match fees

were fixed, expenses could be doctored.

There is a story about the Irish Aldershot manager Bill McCracken who, faced with an attempted scam by the lads (who included the likes of Tommy Lawton, Joe Mercer, Cliff Britton and Jimmy Hagan), used to say 'What money? You told me you'd play for nothing!' He was just joking, but it would certainly get the players worried!

Despite the arrival and departure of a galaxy of stars, Aldershot achieved little of note, possibly because the team was constantly chopping and changing. In the 1943–4 season, Notts County called on 132 different players; more established sides like Arsenal needed only 45, with many of their own players, like Barnes, Bastin, Collett, D. Compton, Drake, Lewis, Male, Marks and Scott playing in the bulk of the matches. High scoring games continued; in 1943 Leeds and Newcastle met each other six times and scored 47 goals between them, Newcastle getting 28 of them. The

ABOVE *An Aldershot scroll, signed by some of their famous wartime players, though Matt Busby turned out mostly for nearby Reading, and Maurice Leyland was a Test cricketer.*

RIGHT *Aldershot FC had at various times a vast array of talent available, including the England half-back line of Cliff Britton, Stan Cullis and Joe Mercer.*

LEFT *Decorations will be worn. A group of cheerful sailors on their way to watch football – clearly a morale booster.*

fact that each team called on more than 60 players during the season must have been a factor.

However, there were some very good players around. Youngsters came through like Billy Wright and Jackie Milburn, while established footballers, in the services and playing and training much more than they would previously have done, were at the peak of their powers. Denis Compton reckoned he had never been fitter. Joe Mercer claims he was never tired, and Ted Drake regrets that the war reduced the effect of his prime. Stanley Matthews was nonpareil. Having become 'fascinated with dribbling', *Athletic News* maintained that he was 'unequalled as artist or crowd magnet', and *Picture Post* said he was 'a football equation without an answer'. An England team,

ABOVE *Tommy Lawton heads England's third goal against Scotland at Wembley in 1942. During the war, England fielded teams of outstanding quality.*

RIGHT *Servicemen were admitted to Stamford Bridge at half price, along with the boys and girls. They took full advantage.*

against Wales, had heard that the opposition were solely interested in closing Matthews down, and came up with an unusual solution. They never gave him the ball, using the rest of the pitch as their personal playground.

The England team of the period might be claimed to have been one of the most powerful ever, and much credit should be given to the Welsh

and Scots for matching and even beating them. The most remarkable international of them all took place at Maine Road, Manchester in October 1943. The teams were:

ENGLAND: Swift, Scott, Hardwick, Britton, Cullis, Mercer, Matthews, Carter, Lawton, Hagan and D. Compton.
SCOTLAND: Crozier, Carabine, Miller, Little, Young, Campbell, Waddell, Gillick, Linwood, Walker and Deakin.

Note that the England side could afford to do without the services of the likes of Ted Ditchburn in goal, Leslie Compton in defence (he probably had upset purists by scoring ten goals in a match as centre-forward) and Stan Mortensen, who had made an international debut, in unlikely circumstances, as a Welsh substitute. No dashing goal-scorer Don Welsh of Charlton either, nor Neil Franklin of Stoke, Bernard Joy or Frank Soo, Reg Flewin or Mullen of Wolves. One spectator, a schoolboy at the time, recalled:

The match became very one sided as Matthews turned it on. We had to duck several times to dodge Lawton's flashing headers and violent shots and by 4.40 England had won 8–0, on top of which Raich Carter had shot wide from a penalty at the Platt Lane End. Our kilted friends, who had previously been boasting about how Willie Waddell was going to destroy the English left flank, had left quietly long before the end.

Lawton scored four and Bill Shankly said that, in retrospect, he was relieved not to have been selected. Adam Little, the Scots right-half, had sat for a medical degree the day before, and travelled through the night to play. And these were no joy rides; the FA told players in 1942 to 'make their own arrangements to arrive in Glasgow by ten o'clock on Friday evening. Members of the party are advised to obtain a meal before leaving and to provide themselves with any refreshments for the journey'.

Sportsmen were determined to get their games in, and the public determined to watch them. At Hampden Park, 105,000 watched England win 4–0 in April 1943, and 133,000 watched the game a year later. These figures were above the ground's official maximum capacity. An attempt in Scotland to have Cup Finals which ended in a draw decided on the toss of a coin was, fortunately, rejected. 'We might just as well have tossed up in the first place,' was a typical reaction. Instead, such matches were decided on the number of corners gained – a much more sensible solution than 'shoot-outs' and so on which, however attractive to the media, have no relation to the game as played. In 1943, Rangers beat Falkirk 11–3 on corner kicks after a 1–1 draw. Next year, Falkirk, after there had been no score in the match, won 6–5.

A mixture of compromise and ingenuity, plus a great deal of often unpaid hard work, had provided the basis for a sporting structure to be maintained though the war years.

# THE HOME FRONT: SPORT IN THE SERVICES

THE Army Sport Control Board (ASCB) was formed in November 1918 to 'control the conduct of sports in the Army, in accordance with the strictest amateur principles'. In the Second World War it was understood that 'rules applicable to the strict amateur principles may have to be modified from time to time'. Nonetheless, the ASCB handbook defined a sportsman in a Corinthian manner as one who:

1 Plays the game for the game's sake
2 Plays for his side and not for himself
3 Is a good winner and a good loser, i.e. modest in victory and generous in defeat
4 Accepts all decisions in a proper spirit
5 Is chivalrous to a defeated opponent
6 Is unselfish and always ready to help others to become proficient.

Service games are modelled on the above. If we keep these six points before us, we shall not go far wrong.

The British services used sports as a way of drawing closer together, and inter-service matches were regularly played in a very friendly atmosphere. By 1945 the Army Football Association had contributed nearly £25,000 to the Army Sports Trust Fund, in addition to grants to various charities and relief funds.

The sporting ethos was written large in official behaviour during the war. For example, the code for launching the attack on Monte Cassino in Italy was 'Bradman is coming in to bat tomorrow'. 1943's *Wisden* noted with approval Montgomery's decision to 'hit Rommel for six right out of Africa' and reminded its readers that, while at St Paul's School, he had gained his colours for cricket and Rugby, and in 1905 had taken part in a last wicket stand of over 100 against Merton College when a severe defeat seemed impending.

*Improvisation was often the name of the game ...
both indoors and out.* Punch, *as usual, summed it up.*

*"About time we changed over ends, isn't it?"*

**PRESIDENTS
ARMY SPORT CONTROL BOARD**

General Sir C. F. ROMER
G.C.B. K.B.E. C.M.G.
1933-1935

General Sir H. S. KNOX
K.C.B. D.S.O.
1935-1937

Lieut.-General H. C. B. WEMYSS
C.B. D.S.O. M.C.
1940-1941

General Sir C. G. LIDDELL
K.C.B. C.M.G. C.B.E. D.S.O.
1937-1939

General Sir R. GORDON-FINLAYSON
K.C.B. C.M.G. D.S.O.
1939-1940

Sport helped to keep the men (and women) fit, entertained and competitive. In certain circumstances it had a direct military relevance. Lillywhite's provided skis for an expeditionary force to Norway and archery equipment to improve hand/eye co-ordination for the RAF. Squash was highly regarded for similar reasons and courts were built in many camps. A variety of football was tried out over a field a mile square to teach tactics, but this idea does not seem to have gone far. Racing pigeons were used by the RAF to bring messages from airmen in distress. There was a cull of peregrine falcons to maintain the pigeons' safety and a Communist trade unionist had his loft

LEFT *From* Games and Sports in the Army. *Despite the distinguished and stern-faced Presidents, and the need for battle-hardening discipline, the Forces recognised sport's recreational role.*

BELOW *Boxers on tour to entertain the troops included (left to right) Dave Crowley, Peter Kane, Kid Berg, Major B. Logan and Jock McAvoy.*

RIGHT *At a desert training centre in California, a pigeon is released. Luckily for the bird, it was expected to return only to base, not Blighty.*

BELOW *Racing pigeons played their part — hundreds were 'called up' to bring messages from men who became isolated. Each bomber crewman here has one in his box.*

destroyed because he would not allow his birds to be used in what he regarded as a capitalist war.

Even the most rarefied sports were encouraged: scramble tennis, played by between two and eight players per side, was a game in which all players on either side of the net held some object (such as a quoit ring, ball or medicine ball) which they threw with the aim of grounding it in the opponent's court. The objects were caught and thrown back in a multiple rally until all were on the same side of the net. There was also a game called 'team

*Darts, at home and abroad, were widely popular. This is part of a ten-ton cargo, bought from the publicly-subscribed Dartboard Fund, on its way to France.*

passing', in which points were scored for the number of passes made without interception. Ground handball was also played, using a soccer ball which was propelled with one hand only, and kept on the ground. The size of the pitch depended on the number of players involved.

Which games were actually played depended to a degree on where one was posted. The PTIs would base their routines around the sports they knew best. Sometimes a group of like-minded sportsmen would be posted together. For example, the table tennis star Johnny Leach ran into a crowd of very efficient table tennis players including Jack Carrington, an English inter national and an officer, who gave him and Ron Craydon encouragement and opportunities for

FUN AND GAMES FOR THE FORCES

*The NAAFI was the centre for sports equipment distribution. Even hunting for lost balls could be a pleasure!*

practice sessions soon after he joined the RAF. It was a widely popular sport in the NAAFIs and, for its effects on hand/eye reflexes and general mobility, it was plainly a game to be encouraged. Carrington, Leach and Craydon also performed in exhibition games. Leach sometimes visited the Irish Republic, in civvies, for competitive games, but basically had no wartime competitive experience.

As a radio operator on 24-hour shifts, Leach had time to practise and, almost without knowing it, because of the lack of real competition, he had become one of the world's leading players. Soon after the end of the war he reached the semi-finals of the world championships. The pre-war champion, Richard Bergmann, joined up (even

though he was not yet a naturalised Briton) but found his opportunities much more limited because he was on active service. However, he still came back to be world champion twice after the war. Stars like Victor Barna played exhibitions to earn the odd crust, although most of the money inevitably went to charities.

Physical training and sport had an important part to play in the women's services. There were deliberate programmes, other than sports and games, to make women conscious of the values of physical activity, particularly those who were engaged in confined working areas. PT was not universally popular, especially if it meant getting up at six in the morning. One PTI corporal recalled how she once came back to her room to find all her clothes had been burned. One enthusiast maintains that 'everyone felt better for the compulsory PT', which may be doubted, but she continues by saying that 'men used to enjoy watching us limbering up', which cannot be doubted.

There were courses designed to train WAAFs to take small groups for exercises and games; the idea was to help those on small stations, who did not have any fully trained PT personnel, to have organised sport. The England women's cricketer, Myrtle MacLagan, recorded that even a rained-off match was a pleasure because the players had a trip to London and ate out. Nonetheless, in 1943, MacLagan led the ATS to bet the WAAF by 141 runs (MacLagan 96) and the WRNS by 210 runs (MacLagan 148 not out). Surely these were performances worth at least a piece of cake. Women played a considerable amount of local competitive sport but some of the most popular games were when they took on the men, particularly at hockey. From Inverness to Sherborne, male teams were laid low. One factor was that, in these games, the women seemed to be of the opinion that the 'sticks' rule – that the stick should not be raised above the shoulder – did not apply, since they were normally smaller. One sergeant, nursing a cut eye,

*Lively hockey action from the women of the ATS. The war brought the concept of a need for womens' fitness away from its association with boarding schools.*

remarked, shortly before Alamein, that if Rommel was faced with a few women's hockey teams he would soon be on the run. Seen a few weeks later, pointing to his scar, he reckoned the women had done pretty well.

There is no doubt that sporting ability conferred certain advantages in the services on the home front. Freddie Mills, the boxer, somehow managed to keep his famous full head of hair. It was said that when they had first shorn him, he had

gone down soon after with pneumonia and this had done the unit's morale no good at all. When asked by one hopeful as to how he managed to keep it, he replied: 'Get into the boxing team, and you'll get away with bloody murder.' This attitude was bound to cause some aggravation. Reg Gutteridge tells of a colonel who told the troops that 'Company A had all the best footballers, Company B the best boxers and Company C all the best cricketers. The welshman, Joe Erskine, no mean boxer himself, was heard to mutter: 'Where do all the bloody soldiers go?'

Douglas Burns MBE was known to have been given off-duty officers' duties and to have been taken off flying duties prior to major services athletics events. His Air Commodore, on his selection for the 100 yards, 220 yards and triple jump for the Bomber Command sports in 1945, advised him to go for a permanent commission to give him even more sporting opportunities. And yet he had already partnered Arthur Wint in a winning relay team and spent two spells at Loughborough Rehabilitation Centre with Dan Maskell, Peter Doherty and Raich Carter, following wrist and knee injuries on the rugby field.

Attitudes to the PTI and their methods varied. There was certainly some resentment, not least for their seeming ability to push off whenever and wherever they liked, and to be paid for it. The gently comic and very popular book *Nice Types* published in 1943 seems to encapsulate popular opinion: Aircraftsman (second class) Plonk was the Everyman of the scene:

Mention of the dread initials PTI invariably fills A. C. Plonk with alarm, loathing, and a strong desire to look too busy for words. For they stand for the Physical Training Instructor – though Plonk thinks that the 'T' should really be for Torture. The Sergeant PTI, with his Assistant Torturer, the Corporal PTI, is the fellow whose

*Fitness was regarded as important for women in the Services. Their confidence was built by new kit in 1941.*

ABOVE *'Nice Types' – Erks in fear and dread of approaching PTIs, at dawn.*

LEFT *Stanley Matthews was a great attraction, wherever he went. This is an RAF match.*

job it is to keep the troops fit, whether they want to be kept fit or not. The PT Sergeant is invariably bursting with rude health and a gloating offensive cheerfulness which is in full spate around dawn, when he meets his victims. They look like a gang of Early Christians waiting in a Roman arena to play opposite a team of Nubian Lions. They feel just like them too – expect that if they had any say in the matter they'd prefer Nubian Lions.

On the other hand, sport certainly gave much pleasure to servicemen. Tom Carter, who played mostly cricket and soccer, reckons he had 'a

marvellous time. The six years I spent in the Army were the best six years of my life'. This was despite being posted to the dreaded 'bloody Orkney'. One of the attractions was the possibility of seeing and playing with great names. The Officers' Mess played the Sergeants' Mess at cricket in the summer of 1943 at a Harrogate holding unit where the PTI was Sam Bartram and turned out two England wicket-keepers, Leslie Ames and Paul Gibb. Matt Busby played in a Scottish quagmire before the referee called the match off, having been struck in the face by the ball, saying 'we must be bloody mad to be doing this'. A 17-year-old, who had played for the local school and church choir, joined a Navy team put together to play an inter-services match. From this humble background he was astonished when the great Stanley Matthews came onto the pitch to play for the RAF. It was moments like this that made service sport that little bit special, because one never knew who might turn out for the opposition, or even one's own side.

# BEHIND THE LINES

JIM LAKER experimented with off-spin in Egypt in 1942. He had previously regarded himself as a batsman and seamer but, on discovering and developing this new cricketing talent, he rapidly found himself playing representative cricket. He had been taking part in a match at a club called El Alamein in Cairo – one of a number of social and sports clubs in the area – against an Australian Services team, and hitched a lift from an officer to get back to base. The officer asked where he had come from. 'El Alamein' was the innocent reply. 'And how are things going there?' 'Well, we missed several chances, and the Australians made a big score,' replied Laker. The officer ordered him out of the car and said he was damned lucky not to be put on a charge.

There is a whiff of the apocryphal about this story, but it says much about the sense of humour of both sportsmen and Yorkshiremen. F. W. Hales, of the RAOC, reckons the club was 'one good thing that came out of the battle'. It had a nice stand, and installed at the front was the bell from El Alamein railway station, which was rung for the start of play. It was used for soccer as well as cricket and featured that unusual Egyptian commodity – grass. Most pitches in the area were of red sand.

Other clubs included one at the Slade Ground and the Abbassia, but the Mecca of sport in the Middle East was Cairo's Gezira Club. This club was a mixture of Lord's, Hurlingham and Ascot. Memories of its social structure vary; on the one hand, it could be seen as 'very democratic... every serviceman was welcomed'. On the other, Gezira was seen as practically 'sectioned off'. As usual, during the war, it was probably a mixture of both, depending on who happened to be be in charge (or paying attention) at the time. Many other ranks, during their time off in Cairo, used to acquire clothes which enabled them to look like officers and so gain entrance to more places.

There is some evidence that barriers were broken down; one NCO given easy duties for organising a successful soccer team, sometimes helped out at the splendid Gezira golf club. Dressed in uniform, he chatted affably with his partner. The golfer wondered how his horses were doing in France. On returning to the clubhouse, the NCO learned that his partner had been Prince Aly Khan. The Aga Khan and King Farouk of Egypt (possibly still shaken by his flirtation with a German alliance earlier) were also in frequent attendance.

Gezira was able to provide not only cricket (for women, too), soccer and golf, but quite high-level horse racing, tennis, hockey and squash. The secret of the grass was that playing areas were from time to time taken out of commission for a couple

*Before the retreat to Dunkirk, a strong Army team played 3 games against the French. Stan Cullis leads out Wilf Copping, Don Welsh, Bert Sproston, Joe Mercer, Reg Allen, Tommy Lawton, Denis Compton, Billy Cook, Albert Geldard and 'Steve'.*

of days and flooded. The addition of nitrate chemicals ensured that it remained healthy.

There were those, of course, who played very little sport while abroad, and watched even less. Those in the Far East had very little time for sport and when they did return to rest and recuperate, many would go down with malaria, beri-beri or dysentery. One serviceman commented on his time there: 'I was involved in amateur theatricals (weren't we all?) and saw only one game (of rugby) played during the whole five and a half years in the Army'. This contrasts with the forthright views of another: 'I can from actual experience emphatically state without fear of contradiction that sport (in my case the games of football and cricket) was responsible for morale-boosting and certainly reduced the strain, stress and the rigors of war'.

Much depended on the unit's mobility, as to whether or not sport was possible. It often felt as if the troops had scarcely put their kit-bags down before they were off again. The most they could hope for, in those circumstances, was an occasional kick-around or a game of cricket with a shovel as a bat.

There was eternal improvisation. This included a very impromptu football match (of the sort much played informally wherever two piles of coats can be set down in a public park) on a beach on D-Day, which was abandoned when the goal blew up. There was also a curious game of baseball in which the pitcher was a captured German gun: it fired either a rubber ball or a milk tin. The striker, 75 yards away, did not know which it was going to be.

Where longer-term postings occurred, more

formal structures grew up. For example, a soccer league was formed from the Helmia, Almaza and Cairo zones, represented by different units of the Army and RAF with each unit adopting the name of a famous club. There were also higher level representational matches arranged. These were major events and the teams were treated like lords. One match, played at Pont de Koubah outside Cairo, showed that it was not always traditional skills that were appreciated, for the higher they kicked the ball, the greater the ovation the players received from the Egyptian crowd.

Sport outside the UK, up to 1944, occupied a sort of no-man's land. Monty was known to be in favour, particularly of boxing, and he helped (via Lillywhites) to provide equipment. However, events depended, to a large extent, on personal and local initiatives.

Certainly, sports proficiency did one no harm. For example, Eric Schnabel found the road to promotion opened to him when he was stationed in Palestine in 1943, because he played hockey. At the end of his first month there he had to appear before the Company Commander for a progress report. The officer, himself a keen hockey player, told Eric that his initial doubts had been removed and that if he kept it up, he should have no difficulty in achieving a commission. So Eric played as much hockey as possible and duly got his commission. No doubt he would have been commissioned in any case, but a certain manipulative adeptness was always an advantage.

Boxing provides some characteristic examples of this manipulation. Bill Coller had a remarkable three weeks in June and July 1943 just after the fall of Tunis when he had three fights, all very different. The first fight was arranged when he walked into an Arab gym and found that a lightweight who had been booked to appear could not make it. Always on the lookout for extra cash, Bill agreed to stand in for him, despite the fact that British servicemen were not allowed to compete in Arab events, in case they were injured.

On the day, he was offered 2,000 francs plus 'other prizes' if he won, which he duly did, in the fourth, against his Tunisian opponent. Then came the shock of the evening. After he was given his purse some Arabs came into the ring carrying two cockerels in a wooden crate, a sack of vegetables, and six bottles of wine. These were the 'other prizes'. Coller kept the purse money and gave the rest to his second.

However, he had broken his little finger on his left hand and could not go sick with it. So he put up with it until his next (official) fight the following Saturday, intending to claim he did it boxing then. His original opponent had not arrived so, although he was only a lightweight, he was put in against a welterweight for the main bout – his opponent had also cried off at the last minute. The warning bells should have sounded then, but he was hammered.

It was only after the fight that he discovered that his opponent was the Californian State Champion.

In the third match, despite his broken finger, Bill was complimented on his left hand by the referee. It was a proud moment for him as the referee was Jack Sharkey, the one-time Heavyweight Champion of the World.

Eddy Jenkinson, who was a secretary with the Amateur Boxing Association, was sent to Cairo to organise boxing for the troops. On one occasion he was obstructed from climbing into the ring during a tournament he was staging by a young man in khaki drill, who was taking photographs on the steps. Eddy angrily told the young man to push off. After the event, the CO sent for him and congratulated him for putting on a good show. He then introduced the young man to Eddy – it was King Peter of Yugoslavia!

And, from Harry Warren, now an international boxing journalist in New York, there is a story about sport saving him from the carnage of the battles at Cassino in Italy, in 1944.

As a boxing champion of the Middle East and of

the Central Mediterranean, I was called from the front line to the rear echelon to receive unexpected orders at the request of the 8th Army Commander, and report to Master-Sergeant Joe Louis, and be part of his boxing circus, to entertain the troops. Several weeks later, I found to my horror that my entire Company in the front line had been wiped out. This was one time that I can thank heavens that I was a boxer, otherwise I'd have been in a box.

Harry Warren's experience illustrates two specific points. First is the general, perhaps fatalistic, belief of the troops in 'the one that's got your number on it'. Sport played an essential part in helping people to cope with the stresses of war: it was a numbing agent because it enabled the forces to forget the war; it was a motivator because it gave the spectators something to cheer and the players something to be involved with, for much of the war was extremely boring for the participants. Second was the authorities' realisation, towards the clos-

*The Alamein Club in Cairo was one of cricket's greener Egyptian fields. Shorts were worn on the pitch, and rather less off it!*

ing years of the war, that sportsmen had their own intrinsic value, apart from being fitness-wallahs and a boost for the unit football team. Certainly, the possibility of turning out on the same pitch as – or watching – professionals had a lasting effect on the memories of many ex-servicemen. Tom Finney features in the recollections of more than most, as he played in locations as various as Wembley, Cairo and Italy. Another great favourite was Wilf Mannion, who eventually found himself organising leave recreation for the pressed troops in Palestine in 1946. The memories and loyalties of so many of these men seem much longer than others, who allowed many sportsmen to be forgotten.

Cricket could sometimes almost reach Test standards, particularly at Gezira, where Australians, South Africans, New Zealanders and some Indians were available for matches. Australian spectators barracking the players added to the big match atmosphere. They watched Hammond, Bruce Mitchell and van der Bijl (both of South Africa), Bert Sutcliffe (New Zealand) as well as Charlie Grove (Warwickshire), Vic Cannings and Bert Pothecary of Hampshire; Yardley and Verity were in Beirut.

Conditions, naturally, varied wildly: on a matting pitch at Ankara, in Turkey, the game failed to stir much native interest. The typical audience was one peasant who frequently sat with his back to the game while the other locals watched the Americans playing baseball in the next field. As A. W. Newsom reported in the 1945 *Cricketer* Spring Annual:

> It was for our own amusement and for that of a sprinkling of British wives and children that we played ... we didn't mind why we swiped, chased and perspired as long as we did so. Most people had either white shirts or white trousers, a few both. As far as I know we only ran to two pairs of proper cricket boots, but one came on the feet of R. J. Parkhouse and travelled in a bag full of miracles of private and personal equipment, which had been with him to play in first-class matches at home in his Glamorgan days ... Alas for us, he played only one game. That one appearance we felt, however, gave us a good bit of tone.

So they played on through the heat and dust helped along by warm Turkish beer; nobody cared when a dust storm blew away the score book.

An even more basic venue was the billiard room of the British club in Karabuck, near the Black Sea. The equipment was a burst ball and a chair leg, and by three in the morning several light bulbs and a window had been broken. Newsom concluded: 'In war, the isolation of belligerents in a neutral country is astonishingly complete, but for an hour or two we can forget it over a game of cricket.'

The mat and the bag became almost totemistic elements for units on the move. The wicket was variable, when under the mat. According to Reg Hovington:

> [The 1st Battalion, the Green Howards] must have established a record for travelling the furthest and playing cricket in more countries than any other unit ... Brigadier A. Shaw, DSO, Commanding Officer from 1941 to 1943, saw to it that one of the Battalion's priorities was to carry and always have available a matting wicket, and woe betide the Pioneer Sergeant if he could not supply on demand the necessary concrete! ... Almost before the Battalion was completely dug in, wickets were being prepared in such unlikely places as a gap in the Sal Forest at Ranchi or in the middle of a seemingly endless desert at Qum.

The joke among other troops was that many of the heavy losses suffered by the Howards during the Italian campaign happened to the Pioneer Platoon, attacked by enemy gunfire while building concrete wickets just behind the line. That mat went with the Battalion to South Africa, India, Iraq, Iran, Syria, Egypt, Sicily, Italy, France, Belgium and Germany.

Another well-travelled set of equipment moved with the 38th LAA regiment of the Royal Artillery in North Africa with A. H. Brodhurst (Cambridge and Gloucestershire) in attendance: 'Wherever we went, there was in the BHQ three tonner our mat and our cricket bag of equipment, and great fun we had in various parts of the desert. Venues included Tobruk, Benghazi and Tripoli.' In Beirut, for a match between England and Australia, the mat was laid at the American Universities football pitch on top of a very irregular batting surface. Later, the cricketers acquired their own ground and quite a good inter-services league was formed. But it was not quite the same as cricket in England: one match was interrupted by a swarm of locusts!

Where the situation was stable, as in Gibraltar from 1942, more organised competition was possible. There the Royal Engineers constructed a matting wicket, a pavilion and a scoreboard, all of which encouraged good cricket. The season ran from May to October, and a league was set up with matches every day. The colony also provided a strong team. As part of the celebrations for VJ Day the Australians took on the Rest of the Rock in a thrilling match, which attracted hundreds of spectators. It was all part of an effort to create an environment which resembled normality.

All games, however odd the circumstances and whatever the level, create winners, losers and – although many Americans and possibly much of the modern generation cannot really grasp it – decisive draws. Exhibition events cannot match this excitement unless they have a name to attract admiration and interest. For example, the French boxing champion, Marcel Cerdan, toured North Africa, and Joe Louis boxed from Reading to Italy – both drew in the crowds.

Towards the end of the war, the Service organisers outside the UK came to appreciate the wealth of talent that they had available to them. At first, with a certain amount of fiddling and cajolery most sport took place with semi-official blessing. It then became a matter of policy. Sportsmen were not only able to provide entertainment for the Allied troops, but they could strengthen loose links with strange groups, such as the Partisans, and thus break down the barriers.

Sometimes national honour was at stake: a British soccer team was instructed to beat a side of Yugoslav Partisans who had been able to defeat some local teams causing, if not alarm, despondency. Mostly the brief was not so explicit, but the professional sportsmen, now directly involved, behaved not only with dignity, but commonsense. There was the original 'match of two halves' in Greece, during a slight pause in their Civil War, when the Greek factions – Monarchist and Communist – agreed to a brief, almost Olympian,

truce. Neither faction would play in a mixed team, so they turned out for 45 minutes each against an Allied team.

Denis Compton became involved with the incredibly ponderously titled Inter Services Sports and Entertainment Committee in India. Compton ran one group, and he enlisted Freddie Mills to help with the entertainment. Mills had organised various boxing events on the way out on the troopship and was still trying to keep reasonably fit. He was pleased to have an old mate, Al Robinson, as a sparring partner in the exhibitions. According to Dennis Brookes:

[Compton was] in great cricketing and social demand when he was stationed in India. On one occasion, when he was batting for the Ranji Trophy at Eden Park Gardens in Calcutta, there was a major riot. The mob stormed onto the ground with every intention of stopping the match. Fortunately, when their leader got out into the middle, Denis just offered him a cigarette from his back pocket and the whole riot dissolved into laughter and requests for autographs.

However, Compton could not control the weather. When he arrived at Chittagong towards the end of the monsoon season in 1944 with two touring football teams, hoping to play an exhibition game for troops on the move to Burma, there was a torrential downpour. The pitch was quickly flooded and the ball bobbed about on the water. Despite this, the teams played on until the bitter end and the crowd remained because they were used to being soaked and this was a special occasion.

Sport behind the lines could vary from the well organised to the totally improvised. At the organised level, in leagues and cups, there was often a trophy to play for, lovingly created by the troops. The donors and presenters of trophies could be highly distinguished: a British unit in Ethiopia put together a league, which included themselves,

*A team photograph for cricketers at the Al Maza transit camp. Sport helped keep soldiers' minds off what the future might hold.*

Ethiopians, Italians, Greeks and Armenians, and the winners were presented with their trophies by the Emperor Haile Selassie himself.

At the other end of the scale came improvised soccer matches against the locals. The British in India and Africa were somewhat taken aback by the fact that their opponents played barefoot. Sometimes the British team was at a disadvantage, as when one side had to swim ashore from their troopship to a local fixture with their boots tied round their necks because they were refused permission to use the life boat. On another occasion the same team played against the Zulus. Although the British played well they could not score the goals they deserved as the Zulus covered exceptionally. One player, becoming suspicious, called a halt to the game and counted their men, to find that one was scampering off the field and 15 remained on it. Under such circumstances, where over-enthusiastic supporters

slipped onto the pitch, a draw was not a bad result.

Much depended on what facilities were actually available. In the Gambia, West Africa, there was virtually nothing, except the sea, which was a venue for canoe-racing among the Africans, swimming and surfing. In this environment darts, snooker, bridge, whist and monopoly were about all that people had the energy for.

Units would sometimes be invited along to watch more obscure sports, such as polo. Even if no-one was much interested in the game many would go to watch, simply for the occasion and the chance to meet others and break from the normal routine. Customarily, a dance might follow big events.

Despite the production of a comprehensive

book called *Games and Sports in the Army*, which even went into such minute detail as to prescribe the correct form of breast stroke, some of the games verged on anarchy. One 'game' played in the grounds of an old country house in Italy involved placing the best vases from the house on a pedestal outside, and throwing a ball at them, to see how quickly they could be knocked off. Elsewhere a sergeant made a boxing ring, placing a boxing glove on two lads and tying their other arm behind their backs and then blindfolding them. The fighters then had to call out and find each other by the sound. If one boxer was unpopular then, unbeknown to him, his opponent would not be blindfolded. One soldier, stationed in Italy, recalls controversy surrounding a swimming gala. There were allegations of cheating when the apparent winners had swum the whole breast-stroke length underwater. Had a copy of *Games and Sports in the Army* been to hand, the controversy would have been resolved by Swimming Law 59 (c) that spelt out: 'The body must be kept perfectly on the breast and both shoulders in line with the surface on the water.'

There was another case of troops falling from the standards expected of sportsmen when a group of soldiers at Sharq-el-Gasch in Eritrea thought a walking stick entrusted to them might be useful as a golf club. A nine-hole course was hurriedly constructed and they used the kernels of the dohm-palm nut as golf balls. In the heat of the afternoon, and much to the mirth of the Sudanese labour force lying in whatever shade they could find, the soldiers hacked their way to the holes, often amid much swearing and throwing their 'club' in disgust. The golfers tried to cover the worst damage to the stick with string and insulating tape. The owner was told that a hyena had chewed the stick and it had only been saved by the bravery of some of the men.

Despite such goings-on, it would be mistaken to assume that such episodes of farce and fraud in sport were central to army life in the war, any more

than *Dad's Army, It Ain't Half Hot, Mum* or *'Allo, 'Allo* are to other aspects. In general, the contrary was true and troops sought with dedication, self-lessness and imagination to arrange events for the benefit of all.

There was, for example, one naval signalman who taught his friends how to play tennis during their time in Aden, making the best use of poor facilities and even worse equipment. They only stopped when all the balls had split. Hockey players near Cagliari in Italy played on a concrete strip on one side of which was the HQ building and on the other, the sea. Sometimes, despite the old camouflage nets which had been put up to prevent the balls going into the water, a high ball went over the netting. An airman had a dog which, on his command, jumped into the sea and retrieved the ball.

The resourcefulness of soldiers was not limited to recruiting dogs to the sporting cause. One hockey enthusiast managed to persuade an airfield construction company to scrape the top surface off a field in Basrah and produce a pitch which was billiard-table flat. He then found 21 other people and proceeded to teach them the game until they were good enough to take on other units, mainly from the Indian Army, often with creditable results. He was equally resourceful in his explanations for his side's defeat at the hands of the RAF near Ismalia. The opposition mentioned that the game might have to be interrupted if a plane wanted to land on the runway, which served as the pitch. He maintained that they spent most of the game looking over their shoulders for incoming aircraft, but whether this excuse can hold for all seven goals conceded must be doubtful.

The half-deck of the *New Amsterdam* was an unlikely venue for a rugby match between England and South Africa, played with a medicine ball. Conversions must have been tricky. Circumstances were rarely as unpropitious as that and much rugby was played by the troops, who often went to great lengths, or distances, for a game: the

ABOVE *Space was limited on HMS* Kent *for recreation, but hockey players, using a rope puck, were able to play under the shadow of the ships' guns. Many other games, apart from deck quoits and the like which were designed first for luxury cruises, were adopted – even a sort of rugby.*

1st Battalion, the Welsh Regiment, based in Palestine in 1940, took to the air for the first time and flew to Cairo to play a New Zealand XV. After a truly magnificent game, they lost 9–11. In some games, representatives of League and Union came together. One match included players from the Union clubs Aberavon, Bath, Rugby, Waterloo, Bradford and Leicester, and League clubs Salford, Halifax, Dewsbury, Bradford Northern and St Helens.

Finally, on the subject of team games, on 4 June in North Africa, members of the 7th Armoured Division played the traditional Eton Wall Game.

The lengths to which servicemen would go to escape the military life and recreate a more peaceful past surely knew no bounds, although it was perhaps the solitary sportsmen – the rowers, cyclists, swimmers and runners – who could best make the break.

Although much of the sport played by troops outside the UK seemed to happen without great organisation, running one of the very popular unit or inter-unit sporting events was a complex business, which was genuinely appreciated both by the participants and the spectators. Such events created a level of team-spirit and co-operation within the unit that could not easily be done in other ways. Many veterans have kept the cuttings

RIGHT *Fencing on board a battleship required little space, and encouraged agility and quick reactions. These were desirable military attributes.*

BELOW *The rugby team at Almaza in North Africa was made up almost equally of League and Union players.*

from local newspapers which reported the events or the programmes from the meetings. The standards achieved were not important as long as it all came off successfully.

Sometimes the organisers are well-known. Admiral 'Froggie' Frobisher put together a hugely popular regatta in the Baltic, when the sailors on a Russian convoy were in danger of becoming bored. The surgeon Lord Porritt encouraged deck tennis on board his ship in a slow-moving convoy round the Cape which maintained morale, provided exercise and entertainment and ensured a good social mix of all ranks, especially of the nursing sisters and medical personnel. On arrival in a desolate area of sand half way between Cairo and the Suez Canal he had to establish a 1,200-bed desert hospital, but encouraged the Royal Engineers to help out by creating a land-based deck court. He also rescued some some cavalry horses from Palestine, which had been demoted to the mundane task of pulling carts and wagons, to create a very active riding school, patronised not only by the hospital's officers, but also by a growing number of nursing sisters. Many found it a pleasant experience, despite the monotony of the desert, as well as being excellent exercise.

There was a gymkhana to celebrate Rommel's retreat, including flat races, novelty events and 'over the sticks' hurdles, which were made from the rough and rather prickly scrub which provided the area's only vegetation. This no doubt encouraged the horses to keep their tails up – and the riders to stay aboard.

One of the most remarkable tales from the war is that of the Buckshee Wheelers. Cycling in the Second World War, except for the Japanese advance on Singapore, and some clandestine operations, was not widely regarded as a military activity. Cyclists themselves tend not to fit easily into slots: they are often highly individualistic, but have a strong flocking tendency.

Staff sergeant Johnnie Walker, who had propaganda responsibilities, used to ride out for pleasure with a middle-aged but very fit Marconi man, Paddy Roebuck, on the sandy tracks of the Nile Delta in the early war years. They came across – hurtling in the other direction – Ken Marshall, a very good track rider. Between them they also had one spare bike. Through Walker's friend, Paul Irwin, the sports editor of the *Egyptian Mail*, they decided to find out if anyone was interested in making use of it, and there was an enthusiastic response.

Bikes, ranging from proper racing machines to those with big Egyptian tyres, were found or borrowed. It was decided to hold a cyclists' reunion in Cairo in 1941 and Irwin managed to advertise the event as far away as the *Palestine Post*. Eventually, by fiddling leave and passes, and by hitching lifts, 150 men turned up. The meeting was hastily shifted to the Cairo Freemasons' Hall (only 30 or so had been originally expected) and many had their first chance to ride a bike or 'talk shop' since they left home. They decided to form themselves into the Fraternity of Buckshee Wheelers. 'Buckshee' derives from the Persian word for a present, and thence to something-for-nothing, or free.

The club grew quickly into a large organisation throughout the Middle East, embracing Benghazi, Tripoli, Alexandria, Khartoum, Jerusalem, Algiers and Baghdad, plus a number of scattered camps, many of which did not actually possess a single bicycle. This deficiency was partially repaired by a two-page article in *Cycling* about the formation of the Wheelers. The business manager Herbert Goodwin persuaded the British cycle manufacturers to send out *gratis* 100 bikes. Three wagons-full arrived outside Walker's office and they were quickly despatched throughout the Middle East. His office also served as sleeping accommodation for riders on leave from the Western Desert.

Runs were also organised by the clubs on bicycles bought, hired or scrounged. Every run was an adventure, as the local bicyles regularly fell

to pieces and punctures and blow-outs were frequent. The roads, mostly sandy tracks made hard by buckets of water thrown on them by gangs of natives and baked by the sun, were not ideal for preserving the bikes in good condition. One Wheeler fell into the Nile, while trying to avoid a camel train, and lived to tell the tale, despite fears of dysentery. Another was nearly arrested after riding across the Sinai Desert and causing confusion among the Arabs. In charge of the police posse was Eric Holroyd, who did not look too harshly on the man, being a Wheeler himself, of the Haifa section.

Perhaps the most remarkable Wheeler of all was The Revd. Charles A. Roach, a chaplain in Baghdad, who cycled from Durban to his parish in Iraq in 1943 when he realised that it was quicker for him to do so than to wait for a ship. Armed only with an air-raid siren to scare off elephants, he cycled 2,000 eventful miles through Central Africa.

*Buckshee Wheelers on the track. A barely even semiofficial group, they attracted great support and the fraternity spread throughout the Middle East.*

*The Times*, in a leading article on Mr Roach's journey, said: 'Such a feat is memorable . . . he has done a notable deed.' This was just one of many such journeys in his life. Now aged 80, he still delivers lectures on them, cycles short distances and swims a minimum of half a mile each day.

Several members, a little less ambitiously, cycled across the Sinai Desert; they were rather bemused by a sign which read 'No halting for the next 130 miles.' Other riders ran across a German patrol in the desert and were told, in perfect English: 'Go away from here. We start shooting in 30 seconds.' No doubt some sort of record was set.

The rendezvous for cyclists going out on a run

from Haifa was Trixie's, the local brothel, which was an ideal meeting place because of its magnificent Roman courtyard. While waiting for their companions, riders popped upstairs for a glass of milk. The story is that Trixie was less than impressed with their sense of priorities, but perhaps they were truly dedicated cyclists.

The Wheelers eventually moved into competitive cycling. The first main event was a 25-mile time trial (12$\frac{1}{2}$ miles out and 12$\frac{1}{2}$ back). The trophy, costing £25, was a silver-plated bully-beef tin, mounted on a pyramid, presented by Lord Kenilworth, president of the Old-Time Cyclists. It was won was Eric Mustill, of the East Liverpool Wheelers, in a time of 1 hour 26 seconds, which was nearly half an hour longer than he normally would have taken, because of a ferocious sandstorm. It was regarded as a most remarkable performance and the trophy is still raced for in the UK.

There were track meetings at the Alamein Club. Over 15,000 spectators watched the racing; prizes were presented by the British Ambassador, Lord Killearn. Egyptians, Syrians and Armenians joined with the British servicemen in the racing and club runs. An ardent supporter of the Fraternity was Farees Bey Sarofeem, an Oxford graduate, whose gifts to the club included a 50-guinea trophy, a cheque for £150 and an open house at his villa 200 miles up the Nile from Cairo.

One of the most remarkable events was the Gezira road-race. A member of the Wheelers' committee, John Pluck, persuaded his friend Russell Pasha, who was in charge of the local police, to close the roads for the race. The journalist Paul Irwin suggested that the Area Commander, Brigadier Crystal, could start the race. Unfortunately, in his column he said that the brigadier *would* start the race. The fact of the race itself, let alone his involvement, was news to the brigadier, so he demanded to see the officer in charge. There was, of course, none.

Walker was the organiser but 'brigadiers don't talk to sergeants'. One of the members was persuaded to see the brigadier to arrange the final details. He received instead a 20-minute dressing-down. After having been given permission to leave, the brigadier called the unfortunate man back – but only to ask at what time he was wanted to start the race!

The race itself was won by Ken Marshall, and there is film of the riders, not used to massed-start road racing techniques, let alone obstacles like traffic islands, making their speedy, if somewhat upright, way round the streets of Cairo. When asked how the Wheelers had got away with it all, Walker replied that it was a mixture of 'nerve and ignorance'. Besides which, once it was done there was nothing that could be done to stop it.

Sport behind the lines in Europe was obviously limited. Cricket was played as far afield as Iceland and Spain, the latter on a not entirely satisfactory polo pitch. As the Germans retreated, contact was made with Dutch cricketers, who were becoming very short of equipment. When the fighting was over, a German burgomeister was instructed to create a square in a suitable field, but, having done so, helpfully arranged the seating all around it. 'What do they think we are playing, —ing marbles?' commented one soldier. Felix Menzel, who had apparently been able, even in the war years, to stage some cricket involving the Dutch and the Indians, re-emerged to organise more cricket in Germany.

Before Dunkirk, British services teams played three soccer internationals against France. There had also been an international rugby match between the British forces and France in Paris; it was the first meeting at this level since 1931, when the French had been barred for alleged professionalism. The British Army won an exciting game 36–3.

At the end of the war several soccer games were hurriedly arranged between the British troops and the locals. Occasionally these games took place so soon after the Germans had left that there were rumours that they had not all retreated, and the games were delayed until the area was pronounced safe. Sometimes it was genuinely dangerous to play, as when an airborne landing group played soccer against the local team at Grave in Holland, after having been isolated in some woods until the 2nd Army cleared a corridor to them. The Army played in their uniforms, the locals in full kit, but the Army still won 5–2, and their arrival was seen by the villagers as a suitable occasion to celebrate.

Similar events were common as the Allies advanced across Europe. Monty, needless to say, organised things, forming a British Army of the Rhine football team 'by Command' at Wuppertal, which included many professionals. Under its various guises, sport 'behind the lines' flourished – albeit in a modified form. From Burma to the Baltic, the forces had shown, by and large, commendable good sense in their acceptance of a mix of casual and organised sport overseas.

# BEHIND THE WIRE

'SPORT stopped us from going crazy' was the opinion held by many British ex-prisoners of war. There were, in Germany, several different sorts of camps. In abbreviation, these were *Stalag*, a central prison camp for Other Ranks; *Oflag*, a central camp for officers; *Stalag Luft*, a central camp for RAF prisoners; *Dulag*, a transit camp, and *Marlag und Milag*, a central naval camp and a merchant navy internment camp. Italy had *campos* and Japan its PoW and internment camps, particularly in Burma, Java and China.

Each prison camp had its own character. In some, prisoners were encouraged to cultivate gardens, while in others, like Stalag IIB, malnutrition was at concentration camp levels. Some guards were brutal and corrupt; they shaved the prisoners' heads, beat them and stole or broke their few prized personal possessions. Others were more tolerant, ready to do deals for a much-wanted cigarette. In some camps, especially the larger permanent ones, sports and games were a central part of life, but elsewhere, particularly when the inmates were recruited for forced labour on a skimpy diet, they were effectively unthinkable.

Boredom and frustration were commonplace. Despite this, escapers, who broke up the routine and brought retribution, were by no means universally popular. Sport was far from being the only means of passing the time: amateur theatricals, music of all kinds (Marlag Nord boasted the entire band of the *S. S. Orama*), reading and self-improvement (up to degree level) and all varieties of gambling games were taken up wherever possible.

'We still find it a bit difficult to fill in time,' wrote a prisoner in Italy in 1942. 'But the chaps here have made packs of cards, dice, Monopoly, Ludo, draughts and dominoes out of biscuit cartons, etc.' It was a case, as he rightly observed, of necessity being the mother of invention. Games such as craps, the ever-present 'housie housie' (now known as bingo), fan tan, versions of roulette, horse-racing with dice – usually on a board, but occasionally with human participants – and even lotteries were all played. This was not, naturally, a total answer to the men's problems. The popular view is coloured by romanticised versions of life behind the wire. In fact, there was thieving, retribution, homosexuality and cases of men effectively committing suicide by throwing themselves at the perimeter.

Pat Ward Thomas, later a golfing correspondent of great distinction, observed that hundreds of young men spent up to five years in confinement, and were still passed fit for flying within a matter of weeks of returning home, which said much for their resilience and adaptability. The prisoners, who had been used to active and exciting lives,

*Boxing – seen here at Stalag Luft III – was easy to stage, and did not need the improvisations of other sports.*

were suddenly thrown together with hundreds of other men for an indefinite period in at best ascetic conditions. This inevitably proved a great strain. Games provided an escape from it all, and the cramped space, barbed wire and lack of proper equipment only served to encourage their efforts.

At first the exercises were fairly rudimentary, consisting of pacing round the perimeter walls – five times round Marlag O camp was two miles – because prisoners were moved with some frequency, not least because the Germans had not finally decided what to do with them over a long period.

Red Cross parcels were central to regular sports activity in the camps. The prisoners' right to receive them derived in part from Article 17 of the Geneva Convention, which stated: 'Belligerents shall encourage as much as possible the organisation of intellectual and sporting pursuits by prisoners of war.' The Red Cross had joined with St John's Ambulance to form a Joint War Organisation Society, and there was much moral and other support from the YMCA. Some camps even held benefit matches to collect for the organisations that had helped them. By 1941 the Red Cross was sending chess, draughts, halma, dominoes, cribbage boards, shove ha'penny, table tennis, poker dice and the wherewithal for all manner of card games to the prisoners. These parcels supplemented the indoor games the men had made for themselves.

The Red Cross believed that sport was a necessity. The prisoners ranged from professional sportsmen right down to those who turned out for enthusiastic if unimportant matches on Saturday afternoons, as well as those who were simply supporters. Games, organised or impromptu, were a far more enjoyable alternative form of exercise than drill or PT. A standard Red Cross sports parcel consisted of:

| | |
|---|---|
| 4 soccer balls | 6 skipping ropes |
| 1 rugger ball | 3 tins of dubbin |
| 4 repair outfits | 4 bean bags (a substitute for |
| 12 waxed laces | rope quoits) |
| 2 cricket balls | 24 table tennis balls |
| (usually | 4 table tennis balls |
| composition) | 2 nets and a pair of posts |
| 3 rounders sticks | 12 waxed threads for repairs |
| 4 pairs of boxing | 12 small balls (4 soft, 4 wooden, |
| gloves | 4 rounders) |

There were also standard team clothing parcels: 30 sets of jerseys, pairs of stockings, shorts and slips, laces, dubbin and 1,444 spare studs. The jerseys were devised to bear some resemblance to the soccer style, but were still tough enough to stand the maulings of rugger. Sometimes the men preferred a mixture of the two which ignored the laws of both games and allowed a free-for-all. Later additions to the packs included cricket bats and stumps, rope quoits, an inflator and a referee's whistle. The latter was presumably not required for that elementary football game mentioned above, variously known as 'roccer' or 'sucker'. A pool was set up in Geneva for the replacement of individual items and specialised equipment for hockey, water polo, basketball and volleyball. Other special items asked for by camp captains could also be sent out.

Between 1942 and 1944 an average of 400 standard units were dispatched each year, as well as many smaller units. On a less healthy note, 6,129,504 ounces of tobacco and 1,464,404,000 cigarettes were sent out between 1941 and 1945. No doubt they were put to various good and possibly questionable uses.

As the Red Cross pointed out, the case enclosing equipment – not to mention all the other supplies – was not simply a crate to be opened, smashed and thrown away. It was strong and long-lasting and could be used to store the equipment. The cases could be put to other uses, too, as with the famous 'wooden horse' at Stalag Luft III which edged ever nearer the perimeter wire while men dug a tunnel under it and diversionary forces leaped over it. This provided one of the greatest escape stories of the war. However, the escape was not actually entirely popular, as the other ranks complained that while they had done the digging the officers had escaped, leaving the vengeful guards to flatten the budding golf course.

However, the string securing the packages probably provided the most use for sportsmen. Not all consignments got through (there was a widespread belief that some never left the British dockyards). Balls were in desperately short supply – they broke up or were hit into forbidden areas; Marlag/Milag Nord, near Bremen, found an expert who could wind the string into cricket balls which, when varnished, apparently moved with some alacrity and diversity. More frequently, the string was used for netting – for tennis, volleyball and cricket practice, behind soccer goals and even for making tennis racquets.

Just as escapers found tailors and forgers among their number (men who probably never knew they had such skills – or wished to indulge in them again), so sportsmen found manufacturers. One Major Lamplough produced a set of quality hand-made leather cricket balls for his camp at Chieti in Italy. Unfortunately, during the ensuing match, five of the six he had made escaped into liberty and he had to start again.

Another minor hero was Sandy MacGregor, at Stalag Luft I in Pomerania. A Red Cross parcel with three footballs arrived there, but a major problem was that the football pitch (about 100 yards square) was surrounded by barbed wire only a few feet from the touch and goal-lines. Balls were frequently punctured, sometimes two in a match, and Sandy was the man who had to repair them. Two more balls appeared from Switzerland and, with as many as 12 games a day being played, Sandy had to take on extra staff. He began to make his own balls by cutting up old knee-boots into panels. Making the bladders was less easy and he had to use those from rugby balls. He also moved into footwear, turning ordinary boots into soccer boots by adding strips of leather to the soles.

Sometimes the problem was to create the sports facilities themselves – moving camp usually meant starting all over again. On arriving at a new camp, Albert Collyer had to organise the levelling of the ground for sport by uprooting the stumps of hundreds of pine trees. Sometimes swimming areas were created, which could be turned into skating rinks in the winter. There was rarely any sign of grass, especially in the north German pine forests, and so the pitches became a quagmire in wet weather. Indeed, a staff of groundsmen could not have coped with the intensity of activity even at the best of times.

In some cases rules and games were adapted to meet the conditions, but elsewhere organisers pleaded for books of rules from the Red Cross to sort out local disputes about interpretation and history.

The competitive urge was very strong. It was easy to find opponents for individual games, but team sports required greater organisation. Occasionally one camp would play another or the prisoners would take on the guards, but usually the teams were made up of those from one hut, rank, service or country.

Competitions also provided an outlet for betting, which greatly increased the level of interest among the supporters. Lager marks (prison-camp bank notes) cigarettes and cheques promising to pay when they all got home were used as currency. Napoleon's dictum that Britain is a nation of shopkeepers is wrong. Britain is a nation of bookmakers and punters.

Albert Collyer, the football secretary at Stalag Luft I, organised five soccer leagues of 12 teams each, as well as exhibition matches on Sundays involving men who had played professional British soccer, or other big matches such as Officers v NCOs or Pilots v Air Gunners. The number of spectators was limited to three rows because of the proximity of the wire. In other camps crowds of thousands watched the matches, reserving their places where necessary. Thus the atmosphere was similar to that of a cup tie in England. For many it was a novel and exciting experience to play in front of a wildly enthusiastic crowd of over a thousand, especially as it included so many friends who would not allow a player to forget his mistakes.

The importance of sports and games can further be judged from a PoW magazine produced by a Yorkshire section in one camp. The authors did a survey of their 173 fellow-countrymen and discovered that only 21 were non-participants, most of whom were prevented from playing by injuries or official duties. Thus, 152 were involved in playing some team sport, as follows:

| 116 | cricket | (76%) |
| 95 | soccer | (63%) |
| 83 | basketball | (55%) |
| 76 | softball | (50%) |
| 65 | rugby | (43%) |

There was also a boxing team available at all weights; hockey and volleyball were played; and half the members played contract bridge. The author believed that this was 'proof positive that Yorkshiremen are sportsminded and keen on keeping fit for the return to Yorkshire and England'. Note the order!

Soccer was usually the main sport, whether in 5- or 11-a-side varieties. Where leagues or cups could be established, teams based themselves on British clubs and, by bartering or 'borrowing' dyes and blanco, knocked up very presentable reproductions of their team's actual kit. (Strip did not then, as now, vary each year). Sometimes the teams represented an area, but they were generally from many regions. Competition was intense. Cups, shields and medals, mostly created from old tins, were awarded and treasured. Stalag VIIB, for a 50-team, room-based competition, also added two barrels of beer to the prize list.

One of soccer's great attractions was that it was simple to stage in almost any conditions. One compound's football pitch, however, had dozens of trees in it, which enabled a player, perhaps not of a specially athletic nature, to hide behind them and suddenly nip out to score a goal, thus adopting the PoW imperative: 'Turn all you can to your advantage.' Rugby was more difficult to organise. This was partly due to the hardness of the potential pitches, but also the relative lack of space for a 15-a-side game. The physical nature of the sport caused great problems too, with many matches breaking out in violence, not too surprisingly,

perhaps, given the frustrations of camp life. So 7-a-side proved more appropriate in many places, and one report to the *Prisoner of War*, the Red Cross magazine for friends and relations at home, used a tournament in 1942 to make a specific point:

> It is quite possible to keep healthy in a prison camp. One inmate of Oflag VIB cites in proof of this the fact that in an inter-regimental 7-a-side rugger competition the winners were an RAF team who had been prisoners for over $2\frac{1}{2}$ years.

There is, perhaps, an element of self satisfaction here from the Red Cross. Naturally, letters openly critical of camp life would not have been allowed out by the German censors, but, at least until the chaos caused by Allied bombing, the Soviet advance and the German retreat, it was often true.

That's the way — Germany is treating her P.o.W.'s

German propaganda made much of the 'comforts' of life in their PoW camps in leaflets dropped to British troops on the Western Front. Though life was nowhere cushy, large permanent camps had reasonable standards of recreational acitivity.

"Boy, what a game!"

Here...

A football match in a German POW camp.

Every camp has its doctors and its own well equipped clinic

*Left:* Allied POW's making toys for their children to be sent home for Christmas via the International Red Cross.

*Right:* Last Christmas every room in the German camps had its mistletoe or a Christmas tree

*Right:* Once a week there are the welcome Red Cross parcels from home. On that day you see nothing but smiling faces.

LIFE IN A GERMAN POW CAMP

Of the other winter sports, hockey was at a disadvantage, because of the lack of space and arid, bumpy pitches. One is slightly surprised that they did not resort to the more primitive – but still wholly demanding – game of shinty.

Some team games flourished in the camps which were scarcely familiar at home, such as volleyball, basketball and softball. Perhaps this was due to American influence as well as the rounders sticks sent by the Red Cross. There was even some reference to netball, now almost exclusively a women's game, but this may be due to confusion with one of the other games.

Athletics tournaments were often organised, sometimes with the help of the captors as at Stalag XVIIID where a German officer gave 500 Marks in prizes for a Whit Sunday sports meeting in 1942, which included 100-, 220- and 440-yard races, field events and six boxing bouts, and was greatly enjoyed by the prisoners. Oflag IVC even staged an Olympic Games lasting a fortnight, with banners and trumpets for the opening ceremony, which created a feeling of international solidarity. The British team may have arrived slightly late but by all accounts were impeccably turned out in whiter-than-white singlets and RAF trousers. And at Stalag 353 an Empire Games was staged, on Anzac day, with ten countries competing.

There was a certain amount of cross-fertilisation of sports between the Americans and the British Empire. The English watched what must have been a relatively decorous version of American football, owing to the lack of body protection available, and realised quickly that under its seemingly meaningless jumble lay a vast variety of techniques. Meanwhile, an exhibition of rugger and soccer apparently elicited the following response from an American: 'Gee, Jim, take a peep at dem dere guys . . . Stoopid . . . it's sheer moider without pads – just like moidering each other – the bums.'

There was some wrestling. Jiu-Jitsu was taught, and could have been part of basic escape training.

Possibly less likely were skiing at Stalag VIIIA, fencing exhibitions by a French *maître* and even a shooting expedition, with a bag of 124 hares. Some officers on parole were occasionally allowed the pleasure of jogging through the woods of delightful German countryside.

Three other sports figured prominently in camp life: boxing, cricket and, surprisingly, golf. Boxing, being relatively simple in concept, was obviously popular. A boxing ring could be made out of odd bits of timber and the like, while the ropes probably came from the ever present Red Cross string. There is no record of any official bare-knuckle fighting and standards could be high. At Marlag und Milag, the boxing schools trained every night; the trainer had been in charge of the London Polytechnic Boxing Club and the star performer was the feather- and lightweight champion of Jamaica. Professionals like Bob Blair and Pat O'Shaye boxed regularly. So great was the enthusiasm that there was even a hospital exhibition by two one-armed boxers. The sport was a great release from ordinary pressures – summed up by a man at Stalag VIIIB who said: 'When I got into the ring, I felt as though I was back in the old days.' He also won first prize – a suitcase. Occasionally old sparring partners would renew acquaintance in a camp and go on to take boxing classes. The organisers of matches were sometimes rewarded by being given an 'easy' job by the senior British officer, such as keeping a graveyard neat and tidy. On the other hand, not all the boxing matches were for morale-boosting purposes. One boxing PoW recalls how he was ordered to put on a fight for the benefit of a German sergeant and his girlfriend. The boxers' reward was one bottle of wine.

Proper cricket is a leisurely affair played between two teams of 11 under a summer sky. The game is, however, vastly adaptable and so it was a favourite in the camps. A bucket and soap box could stand duty as a wicket and there were many local rules: for example, one might score six by hitting the ball onto a roof and yet still be caught out off the same hit. Sometimes strict boundaries were set, beyond which the ball could not go without the batsman losing his wicket – perhaps care had to be taken to avoid a prized flower garden or hitting the ball beyond the fence. However, some of the sentries could be trained as retrievers after discreet coaching – and, no doubt, a certain amount of bribery. 'One or two of them even learned to throw' commented one inmate with a low opinion of German cricketing ability. Tennis balls reinforced by elastoplast or weighted with water were used. A bucket of water was placed where, on a damp English day, there might be sawdust, subtle use of which could produce extraordinary changes in the ball's performance.

In conditions like these, the better players did not necessarily flourish: sometimes the pitch would favour left-handers and good captaincy had to take into account this and other oddities. It was quite possible for a side to attain the doubtful distinction of being dismissed for 0, as happened to the Highland Brigade in one match. Local knowledge was an immense advantage when conditions were unusual and visiting teams could expect to be dismissed very cheaply.

Cricket was immensely popular; at one camp a suggestion that the game might be better at 7-a-side was ruled out because of the numbers who wanted to play. At another camp the prisoners made a concrete cricket pitch in a couple of days, causing a German under-officer to comment that if he had wanted the same amount of work done it would have taken ten years to complete. But sometimes conditions were almost perfect. For a while, the officers' camp at Warburg could even play on a grass wicket and a full size ground with equipment donated by the De Flamingo club of Holland. However, the camp was closed because of the number of escapes.

The cricketers involved in these matches were by no means to be sniffed at; the Schloss Spangeberg could turn out at least three players with first class experience, while a match at Chieti, complete with pavilion clock, operated manually, featured Bill Bowes and Freddie Brown of England and afternoon teas were provided. One story in particular from Donald Jones represents the atmosphere: 'When I entered Sulmona PoW camp in Italy, very low-spirited, I was greeted by the sight of the inmates playing cricket. As a modest but enthusiastic club cricketer, my morale was sent sky-high.' He later had to abandon a planned cricket match when a chance to escape presented itself.

Perhaps the most unlikely sport to succeed in a prison camp was golf, which flourished at, inevitably, Stalag Luft III. The first club was a woman's ancient wooden mashie, but a thing of joy to the few golfers in the compound. Initially, holing out consisted of hitting trees or posts, and the earliest balls were simply spheres of carved pine, string and elastoplast. Interest grew, and greens – or rather 'browns' – began to appear, with tins sunk in not very level ground serving as holes. The old club stood up miraculously, withstanding around 250,000 shots, often in the hands of strong but mightily inexpert players.

Home-made clubs were the immediate answer to the problem, and an American, Lee Usher from Iowa, came up with some made from honed-down hickory ice-hockey sticks, well balanced and strong, notably a number five iron and a putter. The heads were cast in moulds of soap and made from melted down water jugs and stove pipes. Pat Ward-Thomas rightly pointed out that 'the patience, ingenuity and craftsmanship necessary to make an efficient club in this manner without any proper tools except a knife was remarkable. Naturally the Germans took exception to the disappearance of the stove pipes and water jugs, but never took any serious action in the matter, and anyway, nobody cared if they did.'

Three more clubs arrived in the summer of 1943, and golf was played from 8.30 am till dusk. Mis-hits, like the ones through the Germans' lavatory windows, showering the occupants with glass, were inadvisable, but a 'blind' hole over the kitchen was a major test of skill. The windows there tended to suffer too from those who were not good enough.

The art of ball-making continued to expand, although there were worries about the increased weight of the new ones made with rubber centres (from tobacco pouches, air cushions and gym shoes) surrounded by tightly-sewn leather. They could sometimes be hit only 10 or 15 yards short of a real golf ball and were remarkably true in flight. When real clubs and some genuine balls at last arrived, they were generally stripped of their gutta-percha covers and remade with leather to remove any unfair advantage. Sometimes, however, exhibition matches were played between the best players and real balls were used. The course was stretched to 1,500 yards with a gallery of several hundred watching them with the same rapt attention as at a big match in England, ensuring that the players were on top of their game.

The 'browns' were also, by the end of the summer, in excellent condition with the head greenkeeper putting in several hours of work a day. The holes even had adequate bunkers and played true after a few minutes sweeping, particularly after rain. Putting now required skill rather than luck. The Germans sometimes helped to spot over-the-perimeter balls and retrieve them. When winter came one correspondent to the *Prisoner of War* remarked reflectively that 'a few mounds covered in snow are the sole evidence that not long ago there was what we like to call the Sagan Golf Club, where for seven months during a strange summer we found entertainment, exercise and something akin to happiness.'

Sport could entertain people in other ways, with quizzes and lectures (happy the man with an aged and much-thumbed *Wisden*) and reminiscences. It also provided a link with the Germans who came to watch matches ('The best soccer they'll ever see,' was one claim). Matches between prisoners and locals certainly happened in Britain. On the other hand, there is the story of Start FC of Kiev who refused to lose a match against the German Army and were promptly shot (as they had been told they would be), still in their football gear, at Babi Yar. From the German viewpoint the most that can be certainly said is that the amount of sport played by the Britons kept them fitter than they might have been, less fractious and probably not at that time involved in an escape attempt.

In the Far East, opportunities were much more limited. In his civilian internment camp in Wei Shien, China, Eric Liddell, the sprinter recently made famous again by *Chariots of Fire,* supervised many sports activities. He was by then a missionary dressed in a shirt made from his wife's curtains, and would tear up curtains, sheets and table cloths of his own to repair damaged equipment. He taught running techniques, but his main aim was 'to capture the minds and imaginations of those penned-up youths'. Naturally, he would have avoided any form of sport on a Sunday, but when one hockey match, without an umpire, ended in a fight, he broke the principle of a lifetime to umpire a replay 'to keep a handful of imprisoned youngsters at peace with each other'. Sadly, he was to die of a brain tumour in the camp.

In December 1942 *Camp Sports* appeared for the first time as a feature of the Bandeong PoW camp magazine, *Mark Time*, later called *The Mark Time Sporting Weekly.* It included stories about an England v Holland soccer international (England won 4–1) and suggested an international tournament, although the Dutch and Chinese would only be able to field one team each, owing to a lack of players. There was even a sailing club and a regular darts league. The paper ended with a competition to sort out two famous sports players' names from this amalgam of words:

SHAVE BOB JARHLY NICK

The clues were that one had a connection with an Oval and another with a Ring.

*German PoWs in Britain also enjoyed their sport. The great Bert Trautmann, of Manchester City, after being injured at centre half, turned goalkeeper in such a match.*

Men in Thailand and Burma could rarely find the time or energy for such frivolity, but they still managed to play some cricket. In the early days Changi camp in Singapore even provided bats, pads and gloves and true matting on concrete wickets on which the famous Australian cricketer, B. A. Barnett, played. There was a match on Christmas Day 1942 at a Thai-Burma railway camp, Wampo, recorded by E. W. Swanton. The guards suspected that it was a religious event, and thus good for morale, which they had to keep at a low but workable level. A young Eurasian chap called Thoy scored a splendid 100 in five overs. There was a major match at the hospital camp, Nakom Patom, between England and Australia on New Year's Day 1945, with players mostly wearing a scanty triangular loincloth known as a 'Jap Happy'. The Aussies were devastated by the appearance of the English fast bowler Captain 'Fizzer' Pearson of Sedbergh and Lincolnshire wearing boots! The noisy Australian crowd was for once silenced.

The first trip for Mr Swanton as a free man later in the year was to a Thai café, where there was a radio tuned to the BBC. It was an emotional time to hear that at Old Trafford, a previously unknown Australian, called Cristofani, was on his way to a century.

# VICTORY AT A PRICE

WAR in Europe officially ended on 8 May 1945. The jubilant post-war spirit was epitomised by the series of cricket matches, played in the atmosphere of a long-running festival.

Bob Cristofani's finest sporting day came on 22 August 1945. He was playing for Australia in the fifth and final Victory 'Test' match between a team selected from the RAAF and the Australian Imperial Forces, and a team of the best players then available for England, not much short of Test strength. Australia batted first, scoring a meagre 177, so, by taking 5–55 with his leg- and top-spinners, he made a major contribution to holding England to 243. Among his victims was the masterful Walter Hammond who had hit 57 out of 97 in a 70-minute partnership with Hutton.

In difficult batting conditions (the Old Trafford weather had lived up to its damp traditions, but the pitch then began to dry under brilliant sunshine), Australia were in deep trouble in their second innings at 69 for 6. Enter Cristofani, who decided to carry the fight to the opposition, despite the steady loss of wickets at the other end. Eventually he found a dogged defensive partner in R. G. Williams, an opening bowler. Cristofani raced to his century after lunch with a wide range of strokes, including a hooked six off George Pope with a 90 yard carry onto the pavilion terraces.

When he reached his century (101 out of 126 during his time at the wicket) the crowd held up the game to give him a tremendous ovation. Australia eventually succumbed for 210, leaving Cristofani undefeated on 110. England, not without alarms, but sensibly served by the Middlesex men, Robertson and Edrich, won comfortably by six wickets, to square the series 2–2. Cristofani's career, disrupted by the suspension of the Sheffield Shield and his war service, lasted only 18 first-class matches; he nonetheless managed to carve a nook in cricket history. Incidentally, German PoWs were paid three farthings a day to repair bomb damage and generally make the ground presentable. The heavy roller was away, constructing airstrips in the East.

The plans originally laid out for the cricket season of 1945 – much the same as the pattern for the previous five years – originally contained nothing so exalted as Test matches, even of an unofficial variety. The authorities' improvisational skills, having been much honed by their wartime experiences, enabled them to tinker with the various programmes, extending matches here and inserting others there. The Australian Services' teams played a notable part in the season – they were involved in nearly 50 matches. Four hundred and fourteen thousand people passed through the turnstiles at Lord's – an average of 12,000 a day.

The fourth 'Test' at Lord's brought in 85,033 – a record for a three-day game.

There was a certain lack of proportion given to events – the BBC news immediately followed its announcement of the dropping of the Hiroshima bomb with cricket details. Yet the spirit of the summer was well described by the dying Prime Minister of Australia, Curtin, who before the first Test called the MCC:

I cannot forbear tendering my warmest good wishes to English cricket in the coming season, and particularly to all those gracious people who will assemble at Lord's where tradition so richly nourishes and perpetuates our great game.... My sincere good wishes for the reopening of a series which I hope will never again be interrupted.

His wish was achieved and the good spirit between the teams and the sporting attitudes of the captains, Hammond and Hassett, was widely commented upon. After the tour, the manager, Keith Johnson, a member of the Australian Board of

Control, thanked all 'the great cricketing public of Britain'. Despite many of the players having been away from home for a long period, he wrote of their feelings of regret at leaving:

> The matches of the 1945 season will always be a pleasant memory to us, and if we have in any way contributed to the rehabilitation of English cricket, then it was our honour and our pleasure. May I say that we, too, have benefited from these games, and go back home with more experience of cricket and better players.

In truth, though immensely popular, the Australian side was not a particularly strong one, only Lindsay Hassett and Keith Miller making an international impression after the war. Hassett, the captain, was probably overburdened with cares of captaincy and organisation, and averaged only 27.70 in the Tests. Revenge would come with the all-conquering Bradman tour in 1948. Much rested on the dashing, big-hitting and fast-bowling Keith Miller, but although he topped the series' batting averages with 63.28, a back injury hampered his bowling.

Recent Australian PoWs included the tall and elegant R. G. Williams who, although he bagged Hutton four times in the series, never really got among the wickets. He had been in prison for four years, and was eventually awarded the MBE for teaching touch-typing and braille to war-blinded prisoners. Keith Carmody probably came back to cricket too soon; he will always be remembered for his menacing 'Carmody field' of men close to the wicket. R. S. Whitington, troubled with hay-fever, flattered to deceive on this tour, and later turned to journalism. Cec Pepper became a stout figure in Lancashire League cricket and umpiring; Ellis, a left arm spinner, of whom much was expected, played only one Sheffield Shield game on returning in 1945–6; and Sismey, the wicketkeeper, played only one more first class match in Britain, for Scotland in 1952, where he was a professional at Clydesdale.

The Australian International Force had set up base at Eastbourne and the Saffrons ground there was being prepared to help rehabilitate 6,000 PoWs on their way home. Hassett's men had been practising in glorious April weather, but their first match day on 28 April against Bexhill, provided a witches' brew of two snowstorms, lightning, thunder, hail and sleet. Three hours' play was possible; in the last of them Bexhill slumped to 39 for 9; perhaps they alone did not curse the elements. The next match at Eastbourne, against London Counties, was totally wiped out by the weather. Meanwhile, the RAAF opened at Lord's with a solid six wicket victory over the Empire XI, Ellis taking 8 wickets for 21. The match was watched by 12,250 on a glorious summer's day.

The first Victory 'Test' match was just the sort of game that the 70,000 spectators at Lord's had been looking for. Hammond, discharged from the RAF the previous winter because of increasing back trouble, captained England and the dapper Hassett, only a warrant officer in the AIF, captained the opposition. Australia made good use of a green wicket and slow outfield to keep England basically contained. Robertson scored 53, Les Ames 57 and Edrich 45. England had no left-handed batsman in the team nor, for that matter, a left-arm bowler. The opening bowlers, Alf Gover and Colonel Stephenson, were now well into their thirties. In 1936 Stephenson had recorded the best-ever bowling figures for the Gentlemen v the Players at Lord's (9 for 46), but this was nine years later. His figures of 5 for 116 in 36 overs give great credit to his stamina.

The large Australian innings of 455 owed most to a relatively restrained Keith Miller knock of 105, coming in three and a half hours and containing only six fours. R. G. Williams, on the other hand, gave the tail a distinct wag with 11 fours in an innings of 53. England again got the worse of the weather, but worked their way to 294 thanks mostly to a well-judged innings of 84 by Robertson. So Australia needed 107 runs in 70 minutes.

*Wisden* commented that 'the England team deserved praise for doing their part in the speediest manner, changing positions quickly and starting each over without a semblance of delay when the waste of seconds might have meant a drab draw'.

Australia won by six wickets. Hammond stuck to using his opening bowlers, Gover and Stephenson; the latter had not played since 1941 and crucially, perhaps because of the unaccustomed labours, dropped Cec Pepper, who had been brought up the order, at short slip. In the last over, when the clock had moved to seven, Pepper made the winning hit, taking his score to 54 not out. If this was to be the spirit of post-war cricket, the crowd wanted more of it.

There was more excitement at Sheffield for the next match. *Wisden* records it as 'the finest match of the season, played on a natural wicket at the bomb-scarred Bramall Lane ground, memorable for a wonderful hundred by Hammond on the opening day, when the pitch was at its worst, and

*The Victory Tests of 1945 were enthusiastically received. At Sheffield, England fielded Robertson, Hutton, Griffith, Pope, Holmes, Wright, Hammond, Roberts, Pollard, Washbrook and Edrich.*

the successful bowling of Pope and Pollard, each making his first appearance for England'. Pope joined Hammond in a late stand of 107 in 90 minutes against the slow bowlers. Australia's reply was a mere 143 (Carmody 42). England's second innings of 190 was far from convincing; only Hutton (46), Hammond (48) and the wicketkeeper Billy Griffith, appropriately stumped (35), made much of an impression. The Australians required 330 in the last innings and, with the pitch turning more benign and an opening stand of 108 between Whitington and Workman, soon put victory on the cards. However, the vagaries of the pitch proved too much for them and England won by 41 runs, thanks largely to Pollard who took five for 76. 50,000 were present over the three days.

The somewhat unreal nature of the series was demonstrated at the third 'Test' at Lord's. England embarked on a youth policy. Robertson, Pope (who had taken eight wickets in the previous match) and, perhaps more explicably, Errol Holmes were all dropped. In came J. G. Dewes, D. B. Carr and the Hon L. R. White. They had all been schoolboys in 1944, but the experiment was not a success: they made only 47 runs between them and Carr bowled just nine overs, without success. Carr, now a noted cricket administrator, and Dewes played a few Tests after the war, making a very small impact on the scene; and White became the fifth Baron Annaly.

Dewes, then at Cambridge, gave Hutton support for an hour and a half for 27. Edrich and Griffith (another wartime 'unlucky', along with Robertson) put together a resolute stand of 66. England's total of 254 – in weather conditions that appear to have been made variable by a total eclipse of the sun – was at least respectable. But

*At Lord's, the victorious Australians were Carmody, Williams, Pepper, Cheetham, Miller, Whitington, Stanford, Workman, Sismey, Hassett, Cristofani and Ellis.*

Hammond's lumbago meant that he had to leave the field (Griffith assumed captaincy), and Washbrook injured his hand. This left England in some disarray and Australia's modest 194 was sufficient platform for a four wicket victory. Miller made a typically aggressive 71 on the way to this, helped by some poor English catching.

The home team chose more experienced players for the next match. The Australians, now 2–1 up in the series, gave nothing away. A huge crowd on this Bank holiday fixture awaited them every day. Estimates for the total attendance vary between 85,000 and 93,000. Bad weather on the second day virtually precluded a result, especially as Australia built a near-impregnable target of 388 based on 118 from Miller, 57 from Pepper down the order and 59 from Sismey, who injured his thumb. In England's innings, he was not able to keep wicket and his deputy, J. A. Workman, was not up to the task. So Hammond allowed the non-playing Carmody to substitute. This was not unique, but a clear example of the spirit in which these matches were played. Washbrook, with 112, Laurie Fishlock – a player who would have had a much more influential international career but for the war – with 69, Hammond (83) and Edrich (73 not out), paved the way to an English total of 468 for 7 declared, insurance enough against defeat.

After losing the Manchester 'Test' – levelling the series – the Australians moved on to Scarborough for the revived Festival where they destroyed a strong H. D. G. Leveson Gower's XI. The chief innings came from the redoubtable Cec Pepper. Dropped, crucially, by Fishlock at 33, he reached 168 including a remarkable six out of the ground, which cleared the neighbouring houses and landed in Trafalgar Square. On being told of this feat, an admiring but naive in-law commented: 'Very good! Was he playing at Lord's or the Oval?'. The bowler was leg-spinner Eric Hollies who, in 1948, bowled Bradman for a duck in his last, emotionally charged, Test innings. Cec also took six wickets to help the Australians to an innings victory.

The other main match of the season, at Lord's, was England v the Dominions. The latter side consisted of eight Australians, a South African (Fell), a New Zealander (Martin Donnelly) and a West Indian (Learie Constantine) who was chosen, after some hesitation, as captain to replace the sick Hassett. It was his last first class game in England and was a tribute to the high regard in which he was held for his services to cricket before and during the war. In 1969 he was created 'Baron Constantine of Maraval in Trinidad and Tobago and of Nelson in the County Palatine of Lancaster'.

The game itself was a tremendous success; *Wisden* called it 'one of the finest ever seen'.

Pelham Warner said it was 'cricket *in excelsis*. A *joie de vivre* in the batting sparkled through a game which fulfilled any known axiom as to how cricket should be played'. The Dominions batted first. Craig, a left-handed South Australian playing in his only first-class match, set the scene with 56, the inevitable walloping Pepper added 51 and the delightful, left-handed Donnelly with 133 produced a total of 307.

It was not an untoppable target, but the early England batting collapsed; only a stand of 177 between Hammond (121) and Bill Edrich (78) pushed them back into contention with 287. Although Constantine, with 40, and Craig, again, with 32, made important contributions, the Dominions' second innings was about Keith Miller. He hammered the life out of the English bowling, dominated by the leg spin of the solid Hollies and bounding Wright. Did England's reluctance to play leg-spinners and reliance on seamers begin here? Miller blasted his way to 185, with seven sixes, one of which frightened the lives out of BBC commentators before coming to rest on the upper ledge of the broadcasting box.

England required 357 to win and made a noble attempt at it. Hammond was again to the fore, scoring 102 (he was missed twice in the deep early on), which created a record of scoring a hundred in both innings of a match seven times. Support came from Gimblett (30), Billy Griffith (36), Edrich again and J. G. W. Davies, who had been the most economical bowler. The match turned, however, on a magical piece of fielding by Constantine that ran out Phillipson, and the Dominions finally won by 45 runs with eight minutes to spare.

There was a foretaste of the future on 30 June, when the august G. O. Allen, of all people, was given out 'handled the ball' when playing for South of England v the RAAF. The bowler, Roper, had not seen exactly what had happened when he appealed, but the umpire's decision was correct. The Australian captain, Carmody, offered to let Allen continue, but the batsman declined.

Barracking from the 11,000 crowd delayed a restart for some minutes. *Wisden* thought this a timely reminder that 'the rigour of the game' should be firmly re-established.

Both London Counties and the Empire XI completed their wide-ranging fixture lists, although neither club showed any interest in continuing in 1946. At a final dinner at the Lord's Hotel the Empire XI announced that they had raised £15,000 from 238 games. In 1945 Clarke took 135 wickets, bringing his wartime total to 665 for the Empire XI alone. Harry Crabtree made over 4,000 runs during the period – remarkable figures whatever the opposition. For the Counties Joe Hulme and Frank Lee both topped 4,000 runs and Jack Young took nearly 300 wickets.

West of England, normally rather short of penetrative bowling, had an in-and-out season, winning six matches, losing five and drawing seven. The most notable achievement was by 40-year-old R. J. O. Meyer, who was later the guiding light behind that sporting school of excellence, Millfield. Against Weston-super-Mare he scored

*Despite being marred by rain, a memorial match in Leeds to Hedley Verity raised £1,000 for a bed in his name at the General Hospital.*

178 with 10 sixes and 16 fours. A week later against his own county, Somerset, he bowled unchanged for 50 overs to take six for 137.

The various teams available for serious competition at this stage included the RAAF, the AIF, the New Zealanders, West of England, Civil Defence, the Army, the RAF, the improving Navy and the West Indians. Some of the counties were beginning to re-establish themselves: Warwickshire staged another successful festival, despite some bad weather, and Yorkshire played Lancashire in a benefit match for the dependents of Hedley Verity, who had sadly died of wounds in Italy. Altogether 11 matches were designated 'first class'. One, on the anniversary of the outbreak of war, was 'Over 33s v Under 33s', a game with a nostalgic air to its title. Rain badly affected play. The elders prospered through Charles Palmer, who scored 77, J. G. W. Davies (76) and a resounding knock from Pope (84). Arthur Fagg and Willie Watson, a young hopeful who became a double soccer and cricket international, with 131 and 80 not out respectively, helped lift the juniors to a declaration at 421 for seven. A thumping 52 from Trevor Bailey's Dulwich partner, Tony Mallett, from down the order, speeded things up. Mallett also took eight wickets at fast-medium, and a Scot, Robert Hodge, took 5 for 82 in the first seniors' innings.

The high scores emphasised one aspect of the game in 1945: the lack of a penetrative attack. Solid workhorses like George Pope, Laurie Gray, Copson and Pollard were all a trifle long in the tooth. Mallett never quite achieved what was hoped for from him, despite a respectable county career with a year as Kent captain; Bailey was still slim for a quickie (he once toyed with leg-spinning as an alternative); Alec Bedser was in Italy, but was to be desperately in need of an effective partner at the other end.

1945 had been a memorable season, enjoyed by

*And so peace returned. As spectators lolled in the 1945 August Bank Holiday sunshine at Epsom, nothing much appeared to have changed.*

players and spectators alike. However, it was not to prove so much a new dawn as a glorious sunset. The standards of play never again seemed quite the same.

Soccer picked up for the 1944–5 season with much the same system as had applied the year before; despite its complexity, it seemed to satisfy most demands. The North again had two championships, the first of 18 matches and the second varied in number. Huddersfield won the first from Derby, but Derby won the second from Everton. Then came the League Cup, over two legs in the North, won 3–2 on aggregate by Bolton. The South had a single 30 match programme won by Spurs, while Chelsea collected the League Cup in front of 90,000 at Wembley. Receipts were £29,000, of which £13,300 went to the Government in the hated Entertainments Tax. Only ten of the 22 players (three on Chelsea's side) were actually representing their own teams, but in April 1945, with victory on the horizon, nobody seemed to care a great deal. On 2 June Chelsea hosted Bolton in a meeting of the two League Cup winners. The Greyhound Racing Association loaned Stamford Bridge to Chelsea for nothing but they had to pay the match expenses. A dispute over a penalty caused a fracas in the crowd, some of whom spilled onto the dog track and even onto the pitch. After a fight, one of them ran off with the ball. Peace had obviously broken out.

The first international match (although not official) ended in a 2–2 draw between England and France. These were not poor teams; many a manager of a full England squad today would not mind including the equivalents of Laurie Scott (Arsenal), George Hardwick at the back, Neil Franklin (Stoke) and Joe Mercer (Everton) in midfield, and an attack including the incomparable Matthews (Stoke), Raich Carter (Sunderland) and Tommy Lawton (Everton) up front.

There was an agreement that the 1945–6 season would be transitional; the top two divisions were divided north and south of the Trent, and the third

division teams were split into four separate competitions. The wartime League Cup was ditched, but the FA Cup was popularly revived, with the first round proper being played over two legs to boost revenues. Given the slight skulduggery over guest players in the League Cup, they were not permitted in FA Cup matches. Ninety-eight thousand watched Derby County beat Charlton 4–1 in the final at Wembley. Charlton were to take revenge next year. Crowds were large and enthusiastic in response to some highly entertaining play.

Apart from a crowd disaster during a Cup tie at Bolton, when 33 spectators were killed in what was then England's worst soccer tragedy, the most notable feature of the season was a short tour by Moscow Dynamo. Despite the ravages of the war, such were the vast resources of the Soviet Union that some football had still been played at a high level throughout the period. The players who arrived at Croydon in November 1945 were fit, well fed and well trained. The tour, first mooted by Mrs Churchill in Moscow, was controversial, but possibly a sign of the times.

The Soviet officials had a long list of conditions for the FA on arrival, and they did not much care for the Army barracks where they were originally billeted and so they moved to the Park Lane Hotel, owned by the Arsenal Chairman, Bracewell Smith. They attracted a crowd of over 85,000 for their first match, at Stamford Bridge, against Chelsea. Dynamo pulled back from 0–2 at half-time to draw 3–3, and impressed everyone with a style of play which included much use of open space and the beginning of a three-man defensive system. Joe Bacuzzi, who played against them twice, noted their flexible interchange of positions and reckoned them a great side. They then went to Cardiff where they thrashed the home team 10–1.

There followed a bizarre match against Arsenal at White Hart Lane for which the manager, George Allison, scratched together a team which included five of his registered players, but, as it was a midweek fixture, the majority of servicemen

*The Moscow Dynamos soccer tour in November 1945 caused controversy, but none could deny their advanced skills.*

could not be released. Among the guests were Bacuzzi, Rooke, Mortensen and – a master stroke – Stanley Matthews. The match was played in ever-thickening fog and a thoroughly bad spirit. George Drury, according to Bacuzzi, 'whacked a Russian in the fog and got away with it'. In another version of the tale, the Russian referee, Nikolai Latyshev, tried to send him off, but he refused to go; in another Drury did walk off – and promptly walked on again. We shall never know exactly. The

mists of time are as nothing to the fog of White Hart Lane that day. Trofimov of Dynamo, while theoretically having been substituted, stayed on the pitch for some time, so the Russians were playing with at least 12 men – the tale suggests there might have been more. Arsenal's goalkeeper Griffiths of Cardiff was concussed, and at half-time, following an appeal to the crowd for a goalkeeper, Harry Brown of QPR just pipped Sam Bartram onto the pitch. The record book says Dynamo won 4–3, although Arsenal believed that it should have been 4–4 as Rooke equalised after being fouled, only to find that the decision had been given against him.

BELOW *The Oval was set aside as a PoW camp and though never used considerable damage was caused to the pitch. Wartime clutter was soon moved out.*

RIGHT *Pioneers dismantling prison cages at The Oval in 1945. Determined work by the ground staff restored the pitch for the next season.*

Dynamo probably had 12 men on the pitch for a while during their next match, against Rangers at Ibrox, which was drawn 2–2. Another match was planned, against an FA XI, virtually an England team, at Villa Park. Villa had printed 70,000 tickets when it was discovered to everyone's surprise (including, it seems, their own), Dynamo were called home. On their way back, they paused to beat Norrkoping in Sweden 5–0. Whatever the political ramifications of this sudden move, the Russians had left behind images of a new form of fluid and flexible football.

Most sports spent the later months of 1945 preparing for their next seasons; premises had yet to be de-requisitioned, war damage to buildings and pitches repaired. Alec Bedser recalls the devotion of a team of boys and pensioners, under head groundsman Bert Lock, in starting a clear-up at the Oval in October 1945. Although the ex-pected parachutist prisoners had never arrived, the ground had served as an ack-ack gun sight, a barrage balloon and searchlight base, and even as an assault course. Bert Lock had to bring in 45,000 turves from Hoo marshes in Kent to level the playing area. Alec Bedser recalls the groundstaff 'starting at 8am and working until they could no longer see the pitch:

> [Bert Lock] and his makeshift staff somehow got the ground into playable shape. The practice nets had been gnawed by rats. Bert sat in the east stand, often in freezing winds, repairing the nets to have them ready for the new season in early April 1946. I have always thought of him as an unsung hero.

Thus did the wartime spirit of improvisation continue – with shades of the Red Cross string in the *Stalags*.

*American servicemen brought their own games of baseball, football and basketball to British attention. The UK base championship was held at the Albert Hall in 1945.*

Members and players were slow to return from the diaspora: demobilisation was often more myth than reality. The Yorkshireman, Jim Laker, billeted at Catford in South London, joined the local club, whose president, Andrew Kempton, persuaded him to join Surrey. Yorkshire, having had no chance to see the new off-spin wizard who had developed his skills on the Cairo matting, did not oppose this registration. So the great spin partnership, by sheer chance of a service billeting, became Laker and Lock not, for instance, Laker and Wardle.

Travel and other organisational difficulties precluded many major competitions, although Wimbledon managed to stage a series of Inter-Dominions Services competitions in June 1945 which culminated in two matches on Number One Court between the British Empire Forces and the

United States Forces in England; the Service-men of Britain played other Allies. The matches were well attended, both by the general public and guests such as Queen Mary, the Regent of Iraq, the Belgian and French Ambassadors and the sports-minded Mrs Winston Churchill. Dan Maskell, now an OBE for his rehabilitation work at Torquay and Loughborough, played in both matches; as a professional, he would have been banned from playing in a Wimbledon tournament itself.

A huge crowd of 50,000 crammed into White City for the Bank Holiday athletics meeting which featured the Swedes Hagg and Andersson and a restored Sydney Wooderson. The gates were closed, but the locked-out crowd surged past the police cordon and, breathless among those who managed to force their way in, was young Roger Bannister and his father. They saw a marvellous race over a mile, in which Andersson was kept on terms until the final bend, when the Swede broke to win in 4:08.8. This was the first time Bannister had seen the gallant Wooderson, and it gave him a driving inspiration.

There was a fairly ad hoc regatta at Henley on Saturday 7 July over a shortened course, with crews racing three abreast; but there were cups for scullers, all-comers eights and schools. The Oxford and Cambridge presidents resolved to return to the Tideway at Putney in the next spring so that full Blues could be awarded. There had been some opposition to the proposal from the university authorities, presumably from a last hangover of war puritanism.

Speedway, which had been forced into virtual oblivion by the war, made a fast return, albeit in a rather unconventional manner. Johnnie Hoskins, a pioneer of the sport and a wartime radio instructor, determined to break new ground by staging speedway at the home of Bradford Northern Rugby League Club, Odsal. Bradford were already interested in the idea after discussions with E. O. Spence, the Belle Vue general manager. There was one problem: there was no track. The fast-talking Hoskins persuaded Harry Hornby, Bradford's managing director, to go it alone and stage their own promotions.

A track of sorts was constructed quickly, but the

*The 1,000 Guineas at Newmarket – held in 'Victory Week'. Sun Stream (Harry Wragg up) wins from Blue Smoke (E. Smith) and Mrs Feather (A. Wragg).*

ancillaries proved a problem. George Whiteley, Belle Vue's announcer, provided some of the answers with the practical approach so typical of the time. A starting gate was found at Hanley; wiring for the telephone, loudspeaker and lighting systems was found in a local scrap-yard; microphones were built from old wireless parts, and the starting and disqualification lights were motor car headlamp bulbs, painted appropriately. After a furious publicity campaign, the aim was to make 'this immense stadium, this colossal track, the best in Britain, the pride of the North and the envy of the South'. They had been promised First Division status when the League was revived in '46.

The first race, before a crowd of 20,000, was dramatic. All four riders came off on the first bend, which was much sharper than it looked.

The experienced spectators, motor cycle buffs in general and those who were simply curious, quickly came to realise what speedway at Odsal was likely to be all about. The second race almost created a similar tangle and so later heats were more circumspect. Wilf Jay took the hint from early on and won the event with 14 points.

In 1945, riders went wherever they could find a meeting, travelling up to 1,500 miles a week in big American cars. The immense efforts of the riders helped to open up the speedway tracks again. Sometimes the meetings bordered on farce, but the Hoskins publicity machine had brought racing to Bradford and generated huge public interest. It had revealed some of the weaknesses in organisation that needed to be tightened up before the formal opening of the 1946 National League.

# MISSED CHANCES

FOR all t'sheer brass of it, the lack of subtlety and respect, British sport could have done with more people like Johnnie Hoskins. He understood that the clock could not simply be put back to 1939 or earlier in organisational or personal terms. The huge crowds and great enthusiasm obscured the fact that the war had dealt British sport, in both the short and long term, a massive body blow.

It was not simply a matter of death and injury removing experienced and potential players at all levels, but a break in the normal evolutionary process by which both performers and the sports themselves developed. The war produced a number of initiatives which might perhaps have been followed through. However obvious they may seem in hindsight, there were no immediately clear imperatives for major changes in the post-war system.

One who had an entrepreneurial shrewdness was Jimmy Green, the first editor of *Athletics* magazine (now *Athletics Weekly*) who, to avoid the embargo on new publications, started it off with 'Volume II', containing references back to a non-existent 'Volume I'. He noted the deaths of many athletes and war injuries which had put paid to promising careers. The magazine was sympathetic to Cyril Holmes, a 220-yard man of whom much had been expected in the 1940 Olympic Final and who was unbeaten (in unhandicapped races) during the war years, but he had no serious competition to raise his performances. Holmes, on his retirement, seems to have taken the situation equably enough, even praising his Army training of road walks and assaults which, he believed, gave him the stamina which he required to perform at his best. The lack of first class athletes at the premier universities was seen as a blow from which it would be years before Britain could hope to reach pre-war standards. Some felt that the country should not engage in international matches, but wait until the standard had risen once more. There followed a storm of criticism when, in a match against France, only one event out of 12 was won.

In 1948 Britain boldly, and largely successfully, staged the Olympics at a sodden Wembley, but British track and field athletes won few medals and failed to achieve much at Helsinki in 1952. The gloomy prophesies had been justified.

Up to 80 leading British soccer players were killed in the war and many other careers were ruined. Some defied fate and the medicos by resuming when they had been effectively written off. George Hardwick of Middlesbrough, Doug Wright, who had played for England against Norway in 1938, Spurs' amateur wing half blinded for two months, and Jackie Stamps, who played in Derby's 1946 Cup final team, had all effectively been told that their playing days were over after war injuries. However, except in odd cases like Wolves (one of the most successful club teams, who had been able to build on Frank Buckley's youth policies), the guesting and general uncertainty destroyed the continuity needed to build consistently successful teams.

Although it was perhaps a surprise for England to be beaten by the marvellous Hungarians in 1953, it was not a scandal; but losing to the USA in the 1950 World Cup was a different matter. Small wonder that a victim of that defeat, Alf Ramsey, was later to make teamwork a priority for his 1966 Cup-winning side. England, in terms of tactics and skills, had been left behind by the 1950s, and the war had played its part in this.

Cricket, at the top level, perhaps suffered more. E. W. Swanton reckons that about 60 first class cricketers from around the world died as a result of active service during the war. A disproportionate number of these were pre-war university Blues, taking over the role of subalterns in World War One. No fewer than eight varsity skippers were killed during the war.

Undoubtedly the greatest loss was that of Hedley Verity, a captain in the Green Howards, who was mortally wounded while leading an attack on a farmhouse at Catania in Sicily. He lay in a cornfield, urging his men to keep going, but they were forced to retreat and the last they saw of him was with his batman Thomas Reynoldson of Bridlington cradling his head. He died at Caserta on 31 July 1943; news reached England on 1 September, four years to the day since he had completed the humbling of Sussex in that last match before the war. Bill Bowes, a PoW in Chieti, had learned the news earlier from two Canadians who had been moved up from Caserta. Sympathising about the loss of his friend, they reckoned he must have been 'some sort of a guy' and he was buried with full military honours. His grave became almost a shrine: the Bedsers visited it as they

ABOVE *Hedley Verity, who died of wounds in Italy, was the greatest cricketer to lose his life in the war. He was an officer in the Green Howards.*

moved north through Italy later in the war; and, when the MCC stopped at Naples in 1954 on the way to defend the Ashes, Len Hutton put a Yorkshire tie round the headstone. Tall, courteous and thoughtful, with an impeccably high action, his career lasted only ten seasons. Bowling mostly slow-medium, he took 1,956 wickets, heading the averages in his first and last seasons, and was never lower than fifth. In his 40 Tests, he took 144 wickets at 24.37. Robertson-Glasgow, in the *Wisden* obituary, described him as 'the ever-learning professor, justly proud, yet utterly humble'.

Another major War loss was that of Kenneth Farnes, the Cambridge, Essex and England fast bowler, who died in a plane crash, aged just 30. However, he had the height, strength and economical method to add some bite even to a post-war

RIGHT *Hedley Verity's classical upright action. Tall and naturally skilled, he achieved greatness through an application verging on scientific research.*

England attack. He had taken over 700 first class wickets, and was the first household name to die – he had achieved cigarette-card status.

Major Maurice Turnbull, of the Welsh Guards, was shot by a sniper in Normandy while on reconnaissance. He was a great all-round sportsman, who played cricket for England nine times, and hockey and rugby for Wales. He was a more than competent bat – with about 18,000 first class runs at an average of 30 and 29 centuries and he held more than 300 catches. His greatest achieve-ment was, however, as captain and secretary of Glamorgan; his obituarist and friend, J. C. Clay, believed he was the best man of his generation never to captain England. He also, as secretary, set about improving the county's finances. Whereas, in the past, the faithful few had forked out as a gesture in the face of the frequent crises, he now organised events in every town or village and attended each one of them. 'If the figures were known, the number of miles he danced for Glam-organ might be favourably compared with the

LEFT *Kenneth Farnes of Essex, killed on active service in 1941, left England bereft of fast bowling in the immediate post-war years.*

number of runs scored by some of the side!' joked Clay. He did not live to see his county, under the redoubtable Wilf Wooller – then enjoying the hospitality of the Japanese – win their first Championship in 1948. Nor was he given the chance to develop his administrative and imaginative talents at a national level in the drab days of the late 1940s and early 1950s.

It may seem invidious to pick out these few names, as each man's death diminished the game. Yet they served to remind the long-suffering public at home that sportsmen were far from being islands of privilege and safety.

The war killed many established or burgeoning talents – but it also interrupted the training of young sportsmen. Much of a generation went without the consistent practice of basic skills and the regular competition under the eye of experienced seniors that are so vital to a player's development. Improvised games on the sands of Libya or the beaches of Normandy were no substitute for what Eric Midwinter calls the 'learner-cum-journeyman stage'. Facilities were poor; time was short and an effective opposition was often hard to raise. Pre-war players had received this basic instruction, which stood them in good stead when they returned. They tended to be given the first chance, partly for reasons of loyalty but also because they had the vital grounding, even if they were now a little old. Post-war National Service for young men did not help develop their sporting skills, however much playing games in general might be a happy distraction from other duties.

Britain was thus left behind, because other countries managed to avoid the same pitfalls. Some, such as the USA, had greater resources available to them and were able to continue playing sport to a high level, which enabled their

*The death of Maurice Turnbull (Cambridge, Glamorgan and England) cost cricket not only a great player but a fine motivator and administrator.*

sportsmen to gain the experience that their British counterparts lacked. It is also possible that the British had a poorer diet than their opponents as rationing continued for several years after the war.

Even those countries which had been dominated or conquered by Germany came out of the war better prepared for sporting success. This was because the Germans had encouraged sport during the war, enabling athletes like the Czech Emil Zatopek and Fanny Blankers-Koen of Holland to emerge as the stars of the 1948 Olympics. There were three underlying reasons for the German support. The first echoes the reasoning behind allowing games in PoW camps: people kicking balls and running round tracks were presumably not up to much else. They even allowed cricket to be played in Holland and Denmark, despite a few doubts – they wanted the game to be called something else, but could not think what. The players believed that to continue playing cricket was a minor, but successful, act of defiance.

The second reason was an aspect of propaganda, for local and other use. It suggested an essential benevolence that would be magnified when the war was over. Some Norwegian sportsmen, realising that they were being used, apparently staged a short strike. The third reason was based on long-term thinking. These athletes had developed under German tutelage and perhaps they would soon be performing with gratitude in the forever-German Olympics in Hitler's super-stadium. Sport was seen as an arm of policy, perhaps diversionary in effect, but central to the aims of the state and a symbol of its virility. This belief, as part of Marxist theory, was taken up after the war by Central and Eastern Europe.

In Britain the priorities were different. The new Labour Government had been elected with a mandate to create a welfare state, with much emphasis on improving housing and education. Sport came into the official picture only when educational needs could be shown, and it was administered through the Board of Education. The earliest national coaches, such as weightlifter Al Murray and athlete Jeff Dyson, were appointed in this way. The FA, to its credit, felt that it could not demonstrate any real need, as it believed its finances were adequate and that others would benefit more from government aid. Sports like rugby union and hockey were politically opposed to such notions anyway. There was a widespread feeling that it was the government's job to get people working harder, not playing games. It offered little help to the organisers of the 1948 Olympics beyond providing some Spartan accommodation, and was of the general opinion – when it had one – that sport should look after itself.

There was no widespread urge to change the face of sport. It was omitted from the plans to create a new age from the ruins of war. Perhaps the reason for this can be seen in the story of a badminton player who had taken up the game after watching a match while on service. He rose to the level of being doubles champion of the Mediterranean, but he barely competed again after the war. His father had been killed and there were more important things to attend to. Just putting the bits and pieces together was difficult enough

*The great Emil Zatopek of Czechoslovakia spent early years under Nazi occupation.*

· 180 ·

without the distraction of sport. This led to the situation observed by the hockey player, Mary Russell Vick, whereby one could walk onto a pitch to play for England and not know some of the team: some had retired, some had other priorities, and in their place came many who were new to the game at this level.

For many of the minor sports, drawing up a more or less traditional fixture list, choosing teams on the basis of present abilities, let alone staging internationals involving total strangers, was an achievement in itself. Administrators at club and national level had put together scratch teams and published newsletters to boost troop morale, despite career commitments and any additional warwork. For this they mostly received due gratitude. Their experiences meant that they were not inclined to – nor did they see any need for – major reform. A typical case in point was the Women's Cricket Association, which re-established its cricket week between 26 August and 1 September, 1945 at Colwall (that sports-mad Cotswold village) with 68 players and six teams. They might have cut their own pitch with a motor mower but, as they had all played on worse, they decided to continue with things as they were. Perhaps people were now too keen on the spirit of making-do.

However, some of the major sports may be open to criticism for their lack of flexibility and imagination. The war provided a remarkable (if unsought) opportunity to experiment, which revealed that the public would respond eagerly to new arrangements. This was widely regarded as being due to the lack of the 'real thing'. Robertson-Glasgow in the 1942 *Wisden* criticised the exciting one-day games as being 'a snack, not a meal'. And, for those who suggested a competitive version in peacetime, he thought 'they would be the earliest to tire of the experiment. The new clockwork monkey in the nursery, which waves its arms and waggles its head, delights for a few short hours or days. But the children soon return to the older, if more sedate toys, the tried companions in the familiar cupboard.'

He adopts a thoroughly hostile view towards the spectators:

> There will be found those who understand no batting except that which hits the ball far, high, and often; to whom a saving innings of few runs and great artistry is as meaningless as a batch of Hittite inscriptions ... [who] regard the difficult bowler as a nuisance, a fellow that ought to give way to one who can be relied upon for long-hops, full pitches and half-volleys. Such spectators are, frankly, not wanted at County cricket.

He was, to be fair, arguing against one-day games as a substitute for the county championship, and looking critically at three- and two-day proposals. It was a part of a long-running wartime debate about the nature of the game in peace time. He favoured the two-day match, but expected that a three-day system would be readopted: 'Tradition and habit favour it; the chief danger being that tradition so easily degenerates into inertia and habit into self-satisfaction.' The debate spawned numerous committees and sub-committees, with the MCC represented by Stanley Christopherson, the secretary Colonel Rait-Kerr and Sir Pelham Warner from the Club, and the counties by H. D. G. Leveson Gower, Walter Robins and Sir Home Gordon.

Various suggestions were floated, such as a regional competition or a knockout cup (probably over three days), and then dropped. In the end they tinkered with the arrangements for covering pitches and championship points. Even the experiment with eight-ball overs (imagined to favour batsmen), which had been adopted just before the war, was abandoned. It took the down-turn after the post-war euphoria to convince the authorities that a one-day knockout was necessary as well as the Sunday league. Later, more regionalised matches, like the Benson & Hedges Cup, saved the counties from bankruptcy. The amateur/

professional distinction which involved separate dressing rooms, travel and hotels lingered on until 1963; cricket was slow to reflect the post-war change in society. One cannot tell whether cricket would have moved on these lines had it not been for the war, but the game seemed happier returning to the old ways rather than grasping nettles. It was not until cricket was on the brink of disaster that it changed.

Soccer could, perhaps to a lesser extent, be subject to similar criticism. It had established regular forms of competition during the war which, if at times of a rather odd nature, had become increasingly popular. The post-war committee of the FA reported that there were no fewer than eight sub-committees to deal with various matters when hostilities had ceased. The chief decision was to resist the creation of separate third and fourth divisions to replace the existing two third divisions. They were more interested in increasing the numbers promoted to the second division.

The great success of league cups, which provided extra revenue, was ignored. The hated Entertainments Tax was blamed for preventing clubs from spending money on renovating their grounds. The clubs skirted the fact that transfer fees, if skilfully manipulated, could be virtually untaxed, while improvements to facilities were taxed – a wiser approach might have concentrated on this. Apart from staging odd events like boxing matches, football clubs made little attempt to extend the use of their facilities, nor their practical influence in their local communities (as happened with Real Madrid for instance). That sort of thing was regarded as the realm of government; meanwhile they sat back and enjoyed the boom.

What was partially responsible for upsetting this comfortable apple-cart was the professionals' realisation of their market values. This was a direct result of war experiences. Until then, they had been normally better off than the working man. They had, during the war, been able to supple-ment their incomes by playing football and working. On demobilisation, they returned to a wage of £4 a match, a reward which provoked many hard-fought court cases, regarding this and contract and transfer rights over the next 20 years. This more than re-established the differential between their earnings and that of the average working man. The clubs panicked as wages spiralled and gates tumbled. As financial pressures increased new cups, often with a local bias, were set up. These were not dissimilar to the improvisations of wartime, often on a two-leg basis in the early stages.

Flat racing, too, produced its crop of committees. Perhaps as part of a response to anti-racing war puritanism, the Jockey Club in 1941 set up a committee to 'consider the whole future of racing in general and in particular with reference to the encouragement of owners and the greater convenience and comfort of the public'. The committee submitted their report to the stewards, prefacing it with the observation that it was clear that a strong demand for changes prevailed in many directions. In particular, English racing facilities had failed to provide for the general public, as opposed to the regular racegoer. 'Racecourse executives,' it observed, had with few exceptions 'shown little disposition to cater for the individual man or woman outside the fringe of those directly concerned with the business of racing.' The report was detailed, wide-ranging and hard-hitting

The Jockey Club received it and noted that, of course, none of the recommendations could be implemented until after the war. In 1944 a second committee was set up to consider the question of photographing the finish of races; this was in fact set in motion. The first camera to be installed went into action at Newmarket's July meeting in 1947.

At the conclusion of the war, the stewards re-examined the report into the future of racing and issued a declaration of policy in which they stated their intention of providing better and cheaper facilities for the public, increased prize money and a reduction of expenses to owners. Unfortunately, the Club itself could not, in fact, enforce these changes; the courses were independent entities. Although the Jockey Club stewards had the power 'to grant or refuse to grant or renew licenses in respect of racecourses' and to allocate how the prize money should be divided between jockeys, owners and trainers, the stewards do not (as one racing man put it) 'repair the loos in the silver ring', nor do they actually raise the prize money. The reality of the situation gave the courses effective autonomy. More pressing to the Club was the decline, despite all efforts, of the British bloodline *vis-à-vis* the French in particular, who had continued racing and breeding more or less normally during the war. British breeders, who would usually have bought from abroad to improve the stock, were forced to rely on what was readily available.

The great rugby divide re-opened as servicemen returned to civilian life. There was no question of the two codes linking up. This was not unexpected. At the luncheon before the first 'mixed' rugby match in 1943 at Headingley, the Yorkshire Rugby Union President remarked that while the two codes would probably go their separate ways after the war, there could be no line of demarcation between men in uniform. The Rugby League Secretary, John Wilson, said objectively that he did not think that the League and the Union would ever play under one banner.

This was, surely, one of the greatest missed chances. There was no reason why either code should lose its identity. With some imagination, a certain interchangeability could have been arranged. Union could then have avoided later unseemly wrangles about 'boot money', sponsored kit and book-writing, which might ban respected ex-players from even entering Union clubs' premises. League would have been spared the indignity of murky approaches to players it believed might like to join them. So the players, who, for whatever reasons, did not make it in the League, found themselves anathematised, with nowhere to play.

There is, however, a thriving amateur Rugby League which admits former professionals into a limited number of its competitions; presumably this is why even this form of the game lay under the Union's area of prohibition. The demeaning, sad and sometimes absurd saga continued. The captain of the Army Union team in 1943, M. M. Walford of Oxford University, said: 'We are concerned solely with playing rugby, and not whom we are playing with or against'. Is this still the players' view? The Union administrators' determination to return to the *status quo ante bellum* reflected how the 'one nation' apparently created by the war, was – and is – still deeply divided. Ironically, the senior rugby administrator, R. G. Weighill, played in the second and last of those integrated games. A change has taken place recently, however. The 'Free Gangway' agreement by the International Rugby Board in 1986 allows for players to be members of both the Amateur Rugby League and Union. Moreover, the current popular Cups and Leagues in Rugby Union have been most successful, and fears that they would constitute a step towards professionalism have thus far proved unfounded.

# THE UNREAL REALITY

SPORT, by and large, had a good war and yet the record books mostly do not mention these years. Most of the war histories also tend to ignore it, although occasionally there is a page or two on the subject. But sport had an important role to play, and contributed a certain sense of proportion to wartime preoccupations.

The war saw many memorable sporting fixtures, but it is the small, unexpected details which are the most poignant. In his memoirs the cricketer Bill Edrich DFC recalled a Saturday when his squadron was due to play against Massingham, a village side near to its base in Norfolk. That morning, the planes had been called out to assist some shipping off the Dutch coast. Two of them were brought down. Substitute players were found, but the match seemed like a strange dream to him. 'The elms, the roses, the caw of the rooks; these joined the familiar sounds of ball on willow, and the cry of "Owzatt?".' Edrich recalled 'a sudden vision, as real as the other, of a 5,000 ton ship heeling over with pathetic little black figures scrambling up her tilting deck'. It was a hard and exciting game, but then 'one's mind would flicker off to the briefing, and to joking with a pal whose body was now washing in the long, cold tides, and one saw again his machine cartwheeling down, flaming from nose to tail; and then a ball would roll fast along the green English turf and in the distance the village clock would strike and the mellow echoes would ring through the lazy air that perfect summer afternoon'.

'Making do', against all odds, was the spirit of wartime. The headmaster and owner of Dulwich College Preparatory School, J. H. Leakey, evacuated the school to the Royal Oak Hotel at Betws-y-Coed in Wales soon after war broke out. The coming of summer turned thoughts to cricket. A field had been let to the school but it was extremely hard work to create a square with a hand lawn-mower. The outfield was a more difficult problem, since they had no means of keeping the grass down, and were unable to get a haycutter.

> Necessity being the mother of invention, we soon remedied this. On a fine day I had the whole school in a series of radial lines, using the square at the centre of a circle. At a given word, these lines got on their hands and knees and started moving forward, tearing up the grass as they went. This spectacle caused no small amusement in the village.

Despite these efforts, the outfield remained very bumpy. Nonetheless they played some outstanding cricket, with nets set up in the hotel garden. Fixtures were arranged against Rydal Juniors, Ruthin and Llanrwst Grammar School and the

*Artist Anthony Gross captures the feeling of much wartime sport, particularly the relaxation it brought. Indeed the spectators in the seats could not have seen much. Was being there, alive, enough in itself?*

Capel Curig Catholic Approved School among others.

Leakey was rarely at a loss for ideas. When hurrying to the school sports day, he slipped on a stepping stone over the local stream. Parents and local friends had turned up, and his trousers were sodden. However, 'one of the older boys, who was very big for his age, and taller than myself, was wearing a pair of trousers over his running shorts in the manner of University athletes. I called him up, made him divest himself of his precious garment, and getting the boys to make a crowd around mc in the fashion of a rugger match, quickly repaired the deficiency, and was able to view the whole sports while my trousers dried in the sun.'

The important role of sport for troops of all nations was recognised (and used) by their superiors. Mary Russell Vick, long after the war, echoed the thoughts of Mass Observation's interviewees at the start: 'Sport was a relaxation and enabled one to forget the stresses and anxieties of the war.' Denis Howell believes that it filled a major gap: 'The main consideration was that there was nothing else to do. People were working in Birmingham up to six and a half days a week and, with the bombing in 1941–2 particularly, not getting any sleep. It was such a tremendous relief. You really did see then what the social purpose of sport was: to produce a tremendous sense of relaxation for the public, away from the rigours of everyday life. It produced a social cohesion amongst the people in the participation in sport.'

At the higher levels, this was also true. The appearance of major figures at events was not just wall-papering. The status of sport – particularly professional – was enhanced. The 1941 soccer international between England and Scotland saw Winston Churchill being introduced to the players. Seven Cabinet ministers were in attendance: Herbert Morrison, Ernest Bevin. A. V. Alexander, Clement Attlee, Lord Woolton, Sir James Grigg and Lord Leathers, as well as the King of the Hellenes. At Brentford, Herbert Morrison attended an FA XI v Civil Defence match. King Haakon of Norway watched the Inter-Allied Cup final in April 1943, while the England v Scotland match in February 1944 was watched by the King, Princess Elizabeth and Field Marshal Montgomery. A month later, General Eisenhower was the guest of honour at the Charlton v Chelsea London Cup final.

Perhaps these and many other appearances were partly PR exercises, but they emphasised an official recognition of sport's wartime importance. It would have been possible for them not to have gone, expressing some disapproval of trivial goings on. In fact, the opposite was true. There is even a story that Attlee refused to have a teleprinter in his office until he was told it could bring him the latest cricket scores.

The war also helped sportspeople to become more conscious of their intrinsic worth. Admittedly, long after the war, there was an announcement on the Lord's loudspeaker apologising for an error in the scorecard: ' "J. T. Murray" should read "Murray, J. T.".' The post-war professional, however, was now more inclined to stand his ground. The Northampton batsman, Dennis Brookes, has related how Fred Cooper, a Flight-Sergeant who had broken a leg parachuting into Germany, was in 1946 dismissed by

Lancashire.

The secretary said to him, 'Now then, Cooper, I'm afraid you'll have to collect your cards', only to receive the reply, 'Thank you very much, Howard'. So Rupert Howard said, 'Are you aware that my name is Major Howard?' and Freddie said, 'I'll tell thee what, Major – thee call me Flight-Sergeant Cooper and I'll call thee Major Howard'.

He also tells how the formidable Private Dick Pollard, taking part in a charity match, was pulled up by Major Frank Prentice for failing to salute him.

Dick just showed him his fist and said, 'I've a damn good mind to salute you with this, but in any case God help you when I get you up at the other end at Old Trafford after the war.'

For some of the younger players, war service had helped to increase their general confidence on the pitch. 'You grow up rather quickly in those circumstances', remarked Worcester and England opener Don Kenyon. And there were plenty of opportunities to perform. Prior to his demobilisation, he was playing virtually non-stop, for Northern Command, Eastern Command and various RAF sides. He also recalled that there was, after the war, a certain amount of factionalism in the rickety wooden pro's dressing room at Worcester between the old timers, who had lost six years of their careers, and the precociously confident newcomers. Trevor Bailey had also played a great deal of cricket prior to de-mob. His understanding Marines CO looked at the fixtures for the end of 1945 and said, 'What you really want, Bailey, is to disappear until October, but you will appreciate that I cannot authorise a leave allowance.' Such was the pragmatism of sport in the Second World War.

When Sutton United (of the GM Vauxhall Conference) beat Coventry City (fifth in the first division) in a third round FA Cup tie in January

1989, their erudite manager, Barrie Williams, felt moved to quote from Kipling:

> It ain't the individual
> Not the army as a whole
> It's the everlasting teamwork
> Of every blooming soul.

That result itself would stand the test against many of the oddities of wartime football. The sentiment of the verse expresses exactly the role of sport in the Second World War. Individuals of great character there certainly were: Busby, Matthews, Swift ('the finest English goalkeeper who ever graced a net'), Compton, Edrich, Hutton, Hammond and Mills; Bowes and Brown in the PoW camps.

But it was a wider effort, most of the participants probably never thought of themselves as a team in general; that would have been too abstract, too elevated. They would usually have preferred to be somewhere else, doing something else. And yet, to make the best of a frequently almost impossible world: 'We always carried our boots, wherever we went.'

# SOURCES AND FURTHER READING

Two books, on cricket and football, have so far been published concerning sport exclusively in wartime: *The Lost Seasons* and *Soccer at War*.

Cricket:

*The Lost Seasons*, Eric Midwinter, Methuen 1987, is a review of the main matches and person- alities, which puts cricket into a wider perspec- tive of social activity in sport and entertainment.

*Wisden Cricketers' Almanack*, eds 78–83, Sporting Handbooks, provides detailed scores and in- formed opinions about the present state and possible future arrangements of the game, as do current editions of *The Cricketer* magazine.

Personal memoirs and biographies include:

*Len Hutton*, Gerald Howat, Heinemann 1988

*Wickets, Catches and the Odd Run*, Trevor Bailey, Collins/Willow 1986

*Twin Ambitions*, Alec Bedser, Stanley Paul 1986

*Sort of a Cricket Person*, E. W. Swanton, Collins 1972

*Harold Gimblett*, David Foot, W. H. Allen 1984

*Cricket and All That*, W. J. Edrich and Denis Compton, Pelham 1978

*Gentlemen and Players*, Malcolm Marshall, Grafton 1987

*Laker*, Don Mosey, Macdonald Queen Anne Press 1989

Further background is in:

*Cricket: A History*, Roland Bowen, Eyre and Spottiswoode 1970

*Lord's*, Sir Pelham Warner, Harrap 1946

Reminiscences of Service and PoW cricket abound in the two anthologies *Tales from Far Pavilions* and *Beyond the Far Pavilions*, Allen Synge and Leo Cooper, Pavilion/Joseph 1984 and 1986.

Association Football:

*Soccer at War*, Jack Rollin, Collins/Willow 1985, is a Bible and treasury of statistics and stories that is simply essential.

*Biscuits and Royals*, David Downs, Fericon Press, 1984, contains more about wartime soccer than many club histories, though most carry re- ferences: his is about Reading.

The Army Football Association produced a *Cen- tenary Handbook*, 1988

*A History of British Football*, Percy M. Young, Stanley Paul 1968

Other published works include:

*Flat Racing since 1900*, Ed. Ernest Bland, Dakers 1950

*Epsom Racecourse* and *Goodwood*, David Hunn, Davis Poynter 1971, 1973

*Henley Royal Regatta*, Christopher Dodd, Stanley Paul 1981

*The Oxford and Cambridge Boat Race*, R. D. Burnell, O.U.P. 1954

*Encyclopaedia of Rugby League Football*, Huxley and Howells, Hale 1980

*The History of Army Rugby*, John McLaren, The Army RFU 1986

*Centenary 78* (cycling), N. G. Henderson, Kennedy Bros 1977

*Freddie Mills*, Jack Birtley, N. E. L. 1977

*The Queen's Club 1886–1986*, Roy McKelvie, Stanley Paul 1986

*From Where I Sit*, Dan Maskell, Collins/Willow 1988

*100 Wimbledon Champions*, John Barrett, Collins/Willow 1986

*The Breaks Came My Way*, Joe Davis, W. H. Allen 1984

*The First Four Minutes*, Roger Bannister, Pelham 1955

*The Flying Scotsman* (Eric Liddell), Sally Magnusson, Quartet 1981

*Twenty One Up*, Richard Bergmann, Sporting Handbooks 1950

*Pigeons in Two World Wars*, The Racing Pigeon 1976

*School Errant*, J. H. Leakey, Dulwich College Preparatory School 1951

*The Odsal Speedway Story*, F. J. Knowles, Odsal Speedways

Further background material is in:

*Edwardians at Play*, Brian Dobbs, Pelham 1973

*The Nazi Olympics*, Richard D. Mandell, Souvenir Macmillan 1971

*Sports and Games in the Army*, The Army, various editions, esp. 1942–3

*The Oxford Companion to Sports and Games*, ed. John Arlott, OUP 1975

*This Sporting Land*, John Ford, NEL 1977

*Service to Sport, The Story of the CCPR*, Justin Evans, Pelham 1974

*The People's War*, Angus Calder, Cape 1969

*Prisoners of the Reich*, David Rolf, Leo Cooper 1988

*Women Who Went to War*, Eric Taylor, Hale 1988

*How We Lived Then*, Norman Longmate, Hutchinson 1971

*English History*, A. J. P. Taylor, O.U.P. 1965

*Nice Types*, RAFF and Anthony Armstrong, Methuen 1943

*Sport and the Military*, James Riordan, University of Bradford paper.

The chief Archives consulted were at:

*Mass Observation* (the University of Sussex)

The National Museum for Athletics Literature (University of Birmingham)

The Red Cross Society (Barnet Hill, Wonersh near Guildford), especially for *The Prisoner of War*, the official journal of the Red Cross and St John Societies, and *The First £1,000,000*

The RAF Museum (Hendon)

The Imperial War Museum, especially for *Mark Time*.

There is much material in files of publications such as *Picture Post*, *Illustrated* and *Punch*, national and local newspapers, Regimental and other Service collections, school magazines and histories of local sports clubs. The Centenary brochures of Bromley Bowling Club and the Blackheath Harriers, and the (often attenuated) records of Governing bodies (for instance the Amateur Swimming Association) are examples. However, with some exceptions, notably in Bedfordshire, Huntingdon and Devon, most of the material remains more or less uncatalogued and uncollected formally. Such work would seem ideal projects for local history societies and schools. The author would be pleased to hear of any that is being undertaken.

Finally, there are the letters sent to the author as a result of appeals for information and personal contacts. These are invaluable, and acknowledged elsewhere; a selection is being offered to the Imperial War Museum for whatever use is suitable.

# INDEX